Exploring Mathematics

Activities for
Concept and Skill Development

Exploring Mathematics

Activities for
Concept and Skill Development

Kindergarten—Grade 3

Jean M. Shaw
The University of Mississippi

Scott, Foresman and Company
Glenview, Illinois   London

Good Year Books

are available for preschool through grade 12 and for every basic curriculum subject plus many enrichment areas. For more Good Year Books, contact your local bookseller or educational dealer. For a complete catalog with information about other Good Year Books, please write:

Good Year Books
Department GYB
1900 East Lake Avenue
Glenview, Illinois 60025

7 8 9 10 MAL 99 98 97 96

ISBN 0-673-18811-6

CONTENTS

Preface

Mathematics plays an important role in the total development of young children. Useful and pertinent in many situations, mathematics lets children explore ideas related to comparisons of objects and sets of objects. It also allows precise quantification of the number of objects involved, and it facilitates dealing with geometric shapes.

Because it deals with the organization and analysis of data, mathematics also permits the interpretation of trends and patterns as well as the combining and separating of sets of objects. Without question, high-quality experiences in children's early years can extend and deepen their understanding and appreciation of mathematics, thus laying a firm foundation for future work in a variety of fields.

Mathematics enhances the ability of children to communicate by making it possible to convey information about quantity, size, shape, time, and relationship of objects. Children should learn to appreciate the need for using specific mathematics vocabulary as they handle objects and encounter situations with people. They must come to recognize that lacking words like "more," "three hundred," "over," and "square," they cannot communicate with precision; both they and their listeners are likely to become confused. To be meaningful, however, this vocabulary development must be based on work with concrete materials and real experiences.

Wanting to know more about nearly everything around them, young children enter the world of mathematics eagerly. Few have internalized the notion that math is hard or complicated. It is, therefore, an adult responsibility to sustain this enthusiasm for mathematics by providing intriguing materials to work with and by presenting interesting and challenging situations in which to use math.

Effective mathematics teaching and learning begins in the primary grades. It is in the early grades that children build basic understandings about numbers, geometric shapes, measurement, mathematical operations, and relationships between quantities. They build their understanding through meaningful experiences, through verbal interactions, and through practice with a variety of materials. As a consequence, both teachers and children should verbalize or talk about mathematics situations, and they should use math symbols and materials (numerals, diagrams, graphs) to represent those situations. Children gain confidence and deepen their understanding as they practice math skills with varied forms and different situations.

Purpose and Content

Exploring Mathematics presents activities that promote children's understanding of important mathematical ideas while at the same time providing the practice children need to refine their skills in mathematics—the skills needed for quick and accurate problem solving. Although intended as a sourcebook for teachers of children in the primary grades, *Exploring Mathematics* may also be used by parents who want a source of motivating home activities to promote math achievement and reinforce ideas taught at school. The activities, while clearly enriching the standard curriculum, can also be used for meaningful and varied remedial work.

This book deals with areas of school mathematics deemed important by both the National Council of Teachers of Mathematics and the National

Council of Supervisors of Mathematics. It includes a chapter on numeration, emphasizing meanings of numbers as well as work with symbols. Ideas for teaching computation and basic facts are found throughout, and the chapters on problem solving and using calculators provide extended exercise in mathematical thinking and computation.

As they work on puzzling situations, children must decide how to apply the computational skills they have already developed. As they use calculators—modern technological tools for mathematics—children also are encouraged to think mathematically. Working with fractions and graphs furthers children's understanding of numbers and of the relationships between numbers; the chapters on these topics offer several ideas for successful encounters with parts and wholes and with organizing and interpreting data. Finally, to round out this collection of activities, *Exploring Mathematics* presents ideas for involving children in work with measurement and geometry.

To help busy teachers, *Exploring Mathematics* contains ready-to-use teaching aids—worksheet masters, task cards, transparency masters, recipes, designs for manipulatives, ideas for bulletin boards—all carefully keyed to the text that explains their instructional purposes. In many cases, the children can help prepare the materials by coloring and cutting them out, and then they can keep the visuals and manipulatives—essential for successful learning—for subsequent use.

Each activity is written in a standardized, easy-to-use format. Introductory information alerts the reader to the potential of each activity. Objectives tell specifically what the children will accomplish. Instructions for preparing and conducting each activity give the teacher a clear idea of what to do both before and during the exercise. A notation about the approximate amount of time needed allows the instructor to plan effectively. A description of how to evaluate the activity offers ideas on assessing children's progress and judging their attitudes. This evaluation is intended to help teachers identify children who need extra help—from the teacher, peers, older students, or at home; those children who need (or want) additional practice should be encouraged to use the activity materials in a learning center environment. Finally, each activity concludes with extension suggestions—ideas for using the activity in other contexts or using it in a different way to add depth and breadth to children's understanding.

Many of the activities in *Exploring Mathematics* are suitable for use with an entire class of young children. Others, intended for use by smaller groups, enhance opportunities for individual attention and interaction. Still other activities can be completed by pairs of students or even by individual children. Most of the activities feature materials and explorations suitable for use in a learning center.

Development of Concepts, Skills, and Attitudes

This book is based on the idea that young children learn best by being actively involved. As they become actively involved in the activities, children use their natural curiosity about numbers, shapes, sizes, and relationships. They readily communicate and share their work with others. In many cases, they experience a growth in self-esteem as they succeed in solving problems through independent work. By offering many opportunities for creative exploration in generating solutions, *Exploring Mathematics* promotes extended learning in sound, positive ways.

The book addresses development of main ideas and building of understanding. Children develop concepts over a period of time, and they must experience, discuss, and work with many different examples before this development can occur. By paying attention to concept development by teaching for meaning, instructors not only save time in the long run but also produce learners who retain ideas and can both apply and transfer those ideas to new situations.

The activities in *Exploring Mathematics* also allow for skill development. Skills are mental or psychomotor activities that people perform quickly and efficiently. Math skills—such as writing numerals, saying number names, using a ruler, and performing computations—are acquired over a period of time with much practice. Children need varied, interesting, involving activities to help them build and sharpen their math skills.

Having a positive attitude about mathematics is essential to effective learning and skill development. Involvement in interesting activities that offer success experiences builds enthusiasm and confidence among young children. Opportunities to share what they have learned and done enhance feelings of pride and competence. Created with the knowledge that children with positive math attitudes perceive numerical problem solving as fun, creative, and challenging rather than dull or impossibly difficult, the activities in *Exploring Mathematics* are clearly designed to enhance children's math attitudes.

A Companion Volume

This book has a companion volume—*Exploring Mathematics: Activities for Concept and Skill Development, Grades 4–6.* Readers who work with older or exceptionally capable students will want to examine that volume as well as this one. The two books share a common organizational format, although the ideas are naturally quite different. Nonetheless, teachers may find several of the chapters in the intermediate-level book pertinent to some children in the primary grades.

Acknowledgments

I gratefully acknowledge the assistance of Charlette Rikard and Shirley Messer in typing this book and the helpful review comments provided by Jennie De Gennaro and Anne Cernak. Thanks are also due to my children, my colleagues, and my students. They inspired, challenged, and encouraged me in the book's development and completion.

JEAN M. SHAW
OXFORD, MISSISSIPPI

1
Getting to Know You: Numbers

Numbers are important! Without numbers and numerals we could not express our ages or our clothing sizes. We might be able to say that one person is older than another, but without numbers we could not express the difference in months or years. People would not be able to discuss the time they eat lunch or tell each other the scores of ball games. Using the telephone or addressing a letter would be an entirely different experience without numbers.

Children learn to work with and understand numbers by manipulating concrete materials and by working with real objects. They learn to associate numbers (quantities) with their numerals (symbols) through much varied practice. Children also need to practice reading and writing number names as words.

The activities in this chapter provide several practice formats for children to use. Each activity involves using counters—i.e., real objects or pictures to represent the numbers involved. As a result, these activities help children build number meanings along with number skills.

PLAYDOUGH NUMERALS

Practicing numeral formation is a sensory delight with this activity. Children also gain measurement skills as they make the recipe.

Objectives: A small group of children will participate in making playdough. Children will use playdough to form numerals and represent numbers.

Materials: Bowl, measuring cup, measuring spoons, flour, salt, alum, cooking oil, airtight container, recipe (Teaching Aid 1.1a), and playdough cards (Teaching Aid 1.1b and c), scissors, laminating material.

Preparing for the Activity: Gather the ingredients in the recipe and the equipment. Reproduce and laminate the playdough cards and recipe.

Approximate Time Frame: 20 minutes for a group to make the playdough; 20 to 30 minutes for all children to work with the dough.

Conducting the Activity: Choose a small group to make the dough. Divide the rest of the class into small groups, and give each group some playdough and several cards. Show the children how to roll the dough into a snake-like shape and then to form numerals. Guide them into placing playdough balls on the shapes to represent numbers. Circulate among the children, encouraging them and questioning them about the numerals they're forming. ("What numeral is this? Show me a numeral with a curvy part. Count these for me. What number comes after this when you're counting? Show me how to form it.")

Evaluating the Activity: Do the children take turns cooperatively? Can they, with guidance, use the measuring equipment? What successes do the children have in forming numerals? Which children can name numerals? Which can count successfully? Consider giving children who need more help in forming numerals some extra practice with playdough or other sensory materials such as sand trays or sandpaper numerals.

Extending the Activity: Make geometric shapes out of playdough. Number paper plates and have the children put appropriate numbers of playdough "food" pieces on the plates. Make playdough numerals activities part of a learning center.

From *Exploring Mathematics: Activities for Concept and Skill Development,* Copyright © 1990 Scott, Foresman and Company.

BUILDING NUMBER-NUMERAL-WORD ASSOCIATIONS

Children need lots of practice associating numerals and number words with the numbers they represent. Provide practice in many different formats that let children use different modalities—sight, hearing, and touch.

Objectives: Children will match numerals, numbers, and number words.

Materials: Paper to reproduce games, markers, scissors, laminating material, paper clips and magnet, dowel, small piece of aluminum foil, tape.

Preparing for the Activities: Duplicate and assemble the games from Teaching Aid 1.2. You may wish to laminate the game pieces, and then write numerals, dots, or number words on them. Doing so allows you to change the numbers as needed. You may also wish to write on the game pieces first, and then laminate the pieces.

Here are the directions for preparing each game:

Clowns and Hats. Duplicate several sets of clowns and hats (Teaching Aid 1.2a). Write numerals or number words on the clowns' collars and ties. Write dot configurations on their hats. Add numerals to the back for self-checking.

Magic Wand. Prepare a magic (magnet) wand by taping a strong bar or circular magnet to the end of a dowel or thick new pencil. Wrap the dowel in aluminum foil, and tape the foil in place with colored tape. Prepare cards (Teaching Aid 1.2b and c) by folding each in half and taping a paper clip inside each "correct" card. In addition to or instead of the cards from Teaching Aid 1.2, you can prepare similar ones appropriate to the level of your students.

Approximate Time Frame: 20 to 30 minutes.

Conducting the Activities: Show the children how to play the games, and then allow them to work independently or in small groups. Circulate among the children, asking them to name numerals or explain what they are doing.

Here are the directions for playing the games:

Clowns and Hats. The children first match the clowns and hats and then check themselves.

Magic Wand. The children sort the cards into two piles—"correct" and "incorrect" cards. Then they check the cards by touching each with the magic wand. The wand should attract the "correct" cards because each has a paper clip inside.

Evaluating the Activities: Spot-check the children's work or encourage the children either to check each other or use the game's self-checking devices. Watch for correct number-numeral associations.

Extending the Activities: Reuse each format, but match basic facts and answers. You can also use the *Magic Wand* format with equivalent fractions.

+ ÷ × − + − × ÷ +

PIPE CLEANER NUMERALS

Young children get lots of kinesthetic practice forming numerals as they work with this rhyming activity.

Objectives: By following the teacher and the rhyme, the children will form numerals out of pipe cleaners. Then they will match their numerals to number cards.

Materials: Two pipe cleaners for each child, construction paper to reproduce pipe cleaner houses, glue, markers, scissors.

Preparing for the Activity: Prepare the pipe cleaner houses according to the directions on Teaching Aid 1.3.

Approximate Time Frame: 20 to 30 minutes.

Conducting the Activity: Lead the following rhyme, encouraging the children to form their pipe cleaners into each numeral shape. Be sure to form your pipe cleaner numerals so that the children will see each one with the correct left-right orientation.

> Let's all have some pipe cleaner fun.
> Stretch it tall and make a *one.*
>
> Let's see what else we can do.
> Curvy, then straight, and make a *two.*
>
> Follow right along with me
> Curve here, and here, and make a *three.*
>
> One pipe cleaner straight. One more.
> It's bent. They make a *four.*

From *Exploring Mathematics: Activities for Concept and Skill Development,* Copyright © 1990 Scott, Foresman and Company.

Straight here and here. Sakes alive!
Curvy here. It makes a *five.*

Now the pipe cleaner is up to some tricks.
Curve it around, and make a *six.*

The top part is straight and even.
The rest bends down to make a *seven.*

Now our numbers are really great.
Lots of curves, and make an *eight.*

Come along, you're doing fine.
Curve it again, and make a *nine.*

When we have nothing at all,
Curve around just like a ball.
Zero is the numeral you will see—
As curvy a numeral as can be!

Place the house cards in a learning center or divide the children into small groups and let each group work with a set of houses. Then decide which pipe cleaner "lives" in each house. The children form their pipe cleaners into numerals and lay them with the correct house.

Evaluating the Activity: Which children form numerals quickly and correctly? Which children place the pipe cleaner numerals with the correct number configurations?

Extending the Activity: Work with the activity for several days until most of the children know the rhyme and can form the pipe cleaner numerals with ease. Then ask the children to form numerals to answer such questions as:

Which numeral means this many? (show three fingers)
Which numeral follows 5 when we count?
Which numeral means one less than 7?

SHOW ME

Every child can participate in this quiet game. You can check the results almost at a glance, thus giving quick feedback to children on the appropriateness of their responses.

Objectives: Children will listen carefully and then respond by selecting and holding up cards to show number meaning and values.

Materials: Construction paper or scrap paper, markers or crayons.

Preparing for the Activity: Cut ten small squares of paper, 5x5cm (2x2 inches), for each child. Pass out the squares to the children, and have them neatly write one of the numerals from 0 to 9 on each card.

Approximate Time Frame: 5 to 10 minutes.

Conducting the Activity: Call out number descriptions like those below. Ask the children to hold up the numeral card that fits each description. Glance around the room and help any children who don't hold up the correct numeral.

Here are some number descriptions you can use:

Show me the numeral that follows seven as we count. [8]
Show me the numeral that goes with this word. [Write the word "seven" on the board.]
Show me the numeral that means this many. [Hold up four fingers.]
Show me the numeral that means two tens and four ones. [24]
Show me a 5 and an 8. Now use these numerals to form the largest two-digit number you can. [85]
Show me one less than 92. [91]

Some children who are unsure of the answers may look at their classmates' selections for help. Since this exercise is for practice, don't make an issue during the game; but do try to identify the children who need some extra help, and then provide that help at a later time.

Keep the game moving quickly. Just five to ten minutes of practice, with everyone on task, will be beneficial. Have the children save their cards for future use.

Evaluating the Activity: Do the children pick the answer quickly and correctly? Which children need additional help? Consider having these children practice showing numeral cards with classmates who demonstrated mastery of the "Show Me" format.

Extending the Activity: Provide written questions or problems on cards, and then let a child lead the game for a small or large group of classmates. Practice answers to basic facts in this version of "Show Me." Ask the children to sort the "Show Me" cards into various piles—odds/evens; numbers 5 and greater/numbers less than 5; numbers in their street addresses/numbers not in their street addresses. When you teach geometric shapes, make geometry "Show Me" cards and use them to drill the children.

From Exploring Mathematics: Activities for Concept and Skill Development, Copyright © 1990 Scott, Foresman and Company.

COUNTERS, COUNTERS, COUNTERS

Using a variety of counters helps young children learn the meaning of number symbols, compare numbers, and understand place value.

Objectives: Children will make counters and use the counters to represent numbers. Children will work with counters to represent operations.

Materials: Choose one or more of the following materials to make the different kinds of counters: 60 plastic drinking straws and ten rubber bands per child, 110 toothpicks and ten rubber bands per child, 120 paper clips and a small piece of posterboard per child, or 110 lima beans and a 30cm (12-inch) square of sturdy plastic wrap and ten rubber bands per child; storage containers (as described in the activities) for each child.

Preparing for the Activities: Gather the supplies to make counters. Have the children help you make one or more of the following types of counters.

> *Straws.* Cut plastic drinking straws in half. Each child should bundle at least ten groups of ten straws with rubber bands and keep ten loose straws. Straws may be stored in large envelopes or in shoe boxes.

> *Toothpicks.* Bundle at least ten groups of ten toothpicks with rubber bands. Keep ten loose toothpicks. Toothpicks may be stored in envelopes or plastic bags.

> *Paper Clips.* Each child should create ten groups of ten paper clips by making either chains or bundles (nine clips hanging from a tenth) and keep ten loose clips. The children then can hang their clips on a 30x10cm (12x4-inch) sheet of posterboard with sections labeled "tens" and "ones."

> *Beans.* Have the children prepare ten bundles of ten lima beans each, wrapping the beans in plastic wrap and securing each bundle with a rubber band. Each child should also have ten loose beans. The bean bundles may be stored in envelopes or small boxes.

Approximate Time Frame: 30 minutes to prepare the counters; 20 to 30 minutes on several subsequent days to work with the counters.

Conducting the Activities: Conduct the following activities (and others like them) over a period of time; one exposure is not enough. Encourage the children to use their counters whenever they need to in their math work. The counters, functioning as concrete representations of numbers, are necessary to build young children's understanding. Cultivate responsible cleanup of the counters by acknowledging and rewarding the children's cooperation.

From *Exploring Mathematics: Activities for Concept and Skill Development*, Copyright © 1990 Scott, Foresman and Company.

Show-A-Number. Duplicate several Show-A-Number forms (Teaching Aid 1.4). Laminate the forms and then write numbers on them with crayon or grease pencil. Let the children work individually, placing the appropriate numbers of counters on the forms.

Show-and-Compare. Duplicate several Show-and-Compare forms (Teaching Aid 1.4). Write other numerals on the number cards if you wish. Let the children work in small groups, taking turns drawing number cards, representing numbers with counters, and placing a $>$, $<$, or $=$ sign between the numbers.

Operations Families. Have the children use counters to show related addition and subtraction facts. For example, have them use seven counters and arrange the counters to show several facts:

$0 + 7 = 7$
$7 - 7 = 0$
$1 + 6 = 7$
$7 - 1 = 6$
$2 + 5 = 7$
$7 - 5 = 2$, and so on.

Let the children record facts on paper or the chalkboard as they represent the facts. Specify a larger number of counters and let the children show several groupings to make the number. For 20, the children could show two groups of ten, ten groups of two, four groups of five, and five groups of four. If the children bring it up, acknowledge that three groups of six plus two extra counters also make 20.

Have the children arrange counters to solve division situations, too. For example, start with 24 counters and see how many groups of two can be made. Record the work: $24 = 12$ groups of two or $24 \div 2 = 12$. Next have the children divide the 24 counters into groups of three, four, and five. Be sure to include some problems with remainders. The children should refer to them as remainders or "left-overs."

Trading Counters. Duplicate several trading frames (Teaching Aid 1.5). Have the children select a problem, place it in the upper part of the frame, and then place the correct number of counters on the left side. To make the number shown on the right, they must unbundle, rebundle, or trade counters.

Evaluating the Activities: Notice the way children handle the counters and how responsible they are in putting them away. Do the children use the correct numbers of counters? Can they represent the problems and record results accurately? Can the children trade counters with understanding? Children who experience difficulty with the counters will need work, over a period of time, with concrete materials that they can manipulate and trade.

Extending the Activities: Use the counters to represent multi-digit addition and subtraction problems. Use paper clips or bean counters to represent numbers up to 1000.

From *Exploring Mathematics: Activities for Concept and Skill Development,* Copyright © 1990 Scott, Foresman and Company.

TOSS 'N' SHOW

Small groups of children roll numbers on number cubes, read the numbers, and then select counters to show the meanings of their numbers. Rolling the cubes adds interest and suspense: What number will turn up next?

Objectives: Children will read numbers and represent number values with counters.

Materials: Construction paper to duplicate the cube patterns (Teaching Aid 1.6), marker, scissors, glue, counters.

Preparing for the Activity: Make one to three number cubes for each group of children. You'll need just one cube for numbers under ten, or up to three cubes for three-digit numbers. Write the numerals on each face of the cube pattern. Children in the second and third grades could use the pattern to make their own number cubes.

Approximate Time Frame: 20 minutes.

Conducting the Activity: Show the children how to roll the cubes, say the numbers that turn up, and arrange counters to represent the numbers. Most groups will be able to check themselves, but you should be available to answer questions and arbitrate disputes.

Evaluating the Activity: Listen to and watch the children to make certain that they read and represent the numbers correctly.

Extending the Activity: Have the children roll two or three digits and then make the largest and smallest numbers they can with those digits. If they roll a 3, 5, and 8, for example, the largest number they can make is 853 while the smallest is 358. You can also have the children add the values they roll or subtract their smallest from their largest value. Or you can have them list five or ten numbers they roll and then put their lists in order from the smallest to the largest number.

NUMBER TREASURE HUNT

Young children enjoy collecting lots of little number cards and gain a learning experience as they sort and compare their cards.

Objectives: Children will find, compare, and sort number cards.

Materials: Paper to reproduce six to ten small number cards for each child, scissors, laminating material (optional).

Preparing for the Activity: Duplicate and cut apart the number cards (Teaching Aid 1.7a and b). You might also add appropriate numbers. Hide the number cards (Easter-egg style) in the classroom or on the playground.

Approximate Time Frame: 10 minutes for the hunt; 10 to 20 minutes for discussion and work with numerals.

Conducting the Activity: Let the children collect as many number cards as they can find, but encourage them to work quietly and cooperatively. Have the children bring their cards to a large group area or to their seats, and direct them to lay out their cards and see what they found. Allow a few minutes for the children to arrange and discuss their cards.

Now lead the children in working with their cards, performing tasks like the following:

Sorting the Cards. The children sort the cards into piles of each number; into odds and evens; into decades (e.g., 30s, 40s, 50s); into numbers more than, less than, or equal to a given number.

Ordering the Cards. The children simply put the cards in order from smallest to largest. If the children have more than one of a given numeral, they can place the extra(s) one above the other.

Finding Cards to Equal Given Sums or Differences. For example, the children could find any pairs with a sum of 12, or any pairs with a difference of 5.

Using Cards to Form Larger Numbers. The children find cards to make the number for two groups of tens and seven ones, or they find the cards to make "three hundred forty five."

Saying Numbers. The children say the numbers from their cards to the group or to a partner.

When finished with these tasks (or others that the children suggest or ones that you develop as appropriate to the topic you are teaching), collect the cards so that you can play the Treasure Hunt game again in the future. Place a pile of the number cards in a learning center so that individuals or small groups will be able to discuss, sort, and work with them.

From *Exploring Mathematics: Activities for Concept and Skill Development,* Copyright © 1990 Scott, Foresman and Company.

From *Exploring Mathematics: Activities for Concept and Skill Development,* Copyright © 1990 Scott, Foresman and Company.

Evaluating the Activity: Do the children sort their cards according to the directions? Can the children read the numbers they found? Do the children work cooperatively in the activity?

Extending the Activity: Use the Treasure Hunt format to work with geometric shapes or words. Let a small group of children work together and graph the results of their hunt.

+ ÷ ✕ − + − ✕ ÷ +

MORE NUMBER-NUMERAL-WORD ASSOCIATIONS

From mice and bunnies to apples that split open to reveal fat worms and on to horses and riders, these activities provide more essential practice in building number-numeral-word associations.

Objective: Children will match numbers, numerals, and number words.

Materials: Paper to reproduce patterns, markers, scissors, laminating material, brads (for worms and apples).

Preparing for the Activities: Duplicate and assemble the games presented on Teaching Aid 1.8a, b, and c.

Here are the directions for preparing the three games:

Mice and Bunnies. Duplicate Teaching Aid 1.8a so that you have at least ten faces and 20 ears. You may wish to use the mice ears or bunny ears or some of each. Color the patterns (or have the children color them), and then write number words on the faces, dot or place-value configurations on the right ears, and numerals on the left ears. Laminate the pieces.

Worms and Apples. Duplicate Teaching Aid 1.8b so that you have at least ten patterns. Color them (or let the children color them), and then write dot or stick configurations on one apple half and number words on the other half. Write a numeral on each worm. Laminate the pieces, and then use a brad to fasten the worm under the apple halves.

Horses and Riders. Duplicate Teaching Aid 1.8c so that you have at least ten riders, hats, and horses. Vary the riders' hairstyles as you wish. Write number words on the horses, numerals on the hats, and number-dot configurations or place-value notations on the riders. Write numerals on the backs of the riders and horses for self-checking. Laminate the pieces.

Approximate Time Frame: 30 to 40 minutes.

Conducting the Activities: Show the children how to work with each game and how to check themselves or check each other.
Here are the directions for playing the three games:

Mice and Bunnies. The children place two ears on each animal and then check themselves.

Worms and Apples. The children count the dots, read the word, and then open the apple to see and read the numeral inside.

Horses and Riders. The children match the horses, riders, and hats; then they check themselves.

As the children work in pairs or small groups, walk around and check on their progress. Offer encouragement and guidance. Occasionally ask a child to explain his or her work, read some numerals, or compare numerals. Ask: Which is more? Which is less?

Evaluating the Activities: Did the children match numbers, numerals, and words correctly and quickly? Could they explain their work?

Extending the Activities: Using the same patterns, have the children match basic facts and answers.

From *Exploring Mathematics: Activities for Concept and Skill Development*, Copyright © 1990 Scott, Foresman and Company.

÷ ✕ − ✚ − ✕ ÷

CHAPTER

1

TEACHING AIDS

÷ ✕ − ✚ − ✕ ÷

HOT WATER PLAYDOUGH

Measure and mix in a bowl:
600 mℓ (2½c.) flour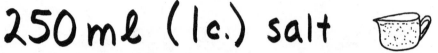
250 mℓ (1c.) salt
15 mℓ (1T.) alum

Add:
60 mℓ (¼c.) oil

Stir in:
375 mℓ (1½c.) hot water

Knead on table top until smooth. Knead in food coloring if you wish. Store in airtight container.

Teaching Aid 1.1a

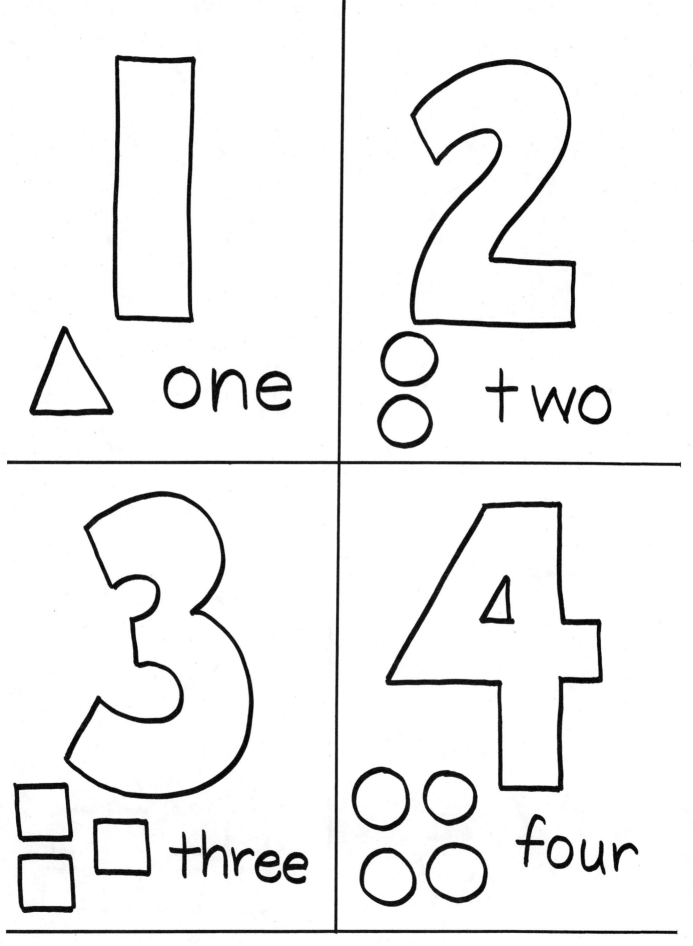

one

two

three

four

Teaching Aid 1.1 b

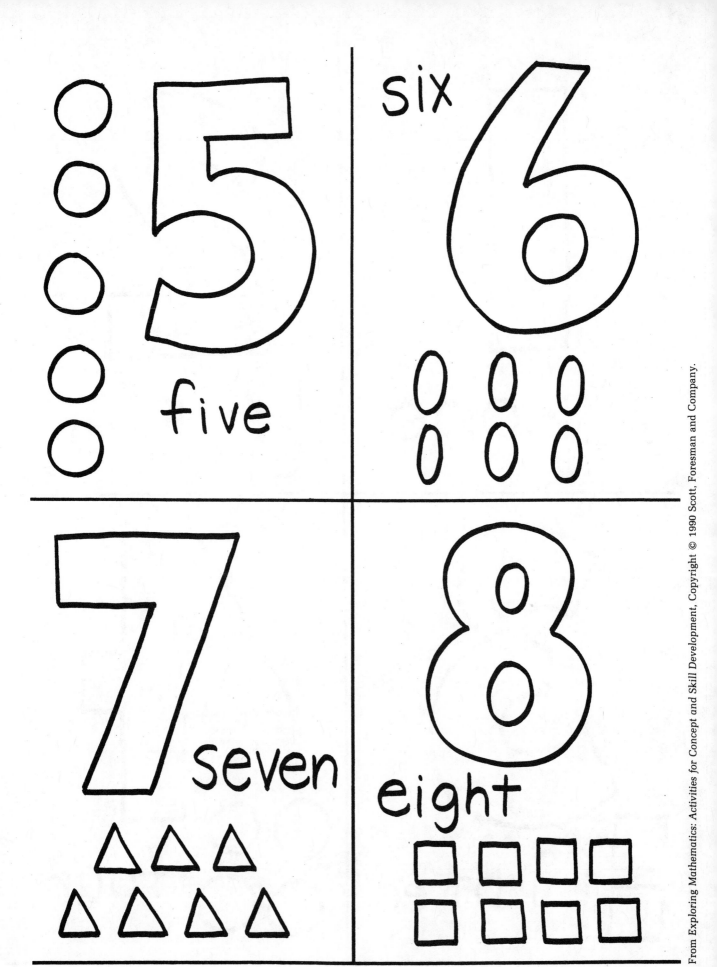

5 five

six 6

7 seven

8 eight

Building Number–Numeral – Word
Associations

CLOWNS &
HATS

Duplicate and color
several sets of clowns and
hats. Write numerals or number
words on the clowns' collars and ties.
Write dot configurations on their hats.
Add numerals on the backs for self-
checking. Have children match the parts.
Teaching Aid 1.2a

Building Number-Numeral-Word Associations MAGIC Wand	
Find all the **3's** Check with the **MAGIC** Wand	
●●●	///
three	5
△△△	two
3	▢▢ ▢▢
2+1	●●● ●●●
0+3	five

the wand lifts the correct cards

Cards for the Magic Wand
Teaching Aid 1.2b

From Exploring Mathematics: Activities for Concept and Skill Development, Copyright © 1990 Scott, Foresman and Company.

Find all the
12's
Check with the
-.MAGIC WAND.-

△△△△
△△△△
△△△△

twelve	9+3
1 ten 2 ones	5+7
HH HH II	13
(dots in circle) ..	21
one more than 11	two
10+2	2 tens 1 one
• • • • • • • • • • • • • •	00000 00000
(rod of ten and 2 units)	ten

Teaching Aid 1.2c More Cards for the Magic Wand

PIPE CLEANER
Numerals

NUMBER HOUSE
Pattern

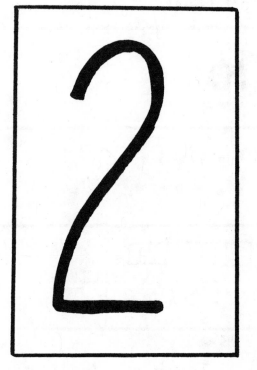

sample numeral card

Duplicate 10 houses, perhaps on construction paper. Duplicate 7 sets of windows on a contrasting color paper. Glue 0-9 windows on the houses. Glue each house to a 15×20 cm (6×9 inch) piece of construction paper. Write the numeral for each house, according to its number of windows, on the back of the house. The children place the appropriate pipe cleaner numeral with each house.

To help children who need guidance forming numerals, make a set of numeral cards writing each numeral in the approximate size it will be when formed with a pipe cleaner.

Teaching Aid 1.3

From Exploring Mathematics: Activities for Concept and Skill Development, Copyright © 1990 Scott, Foresman and Company.

Show the Number of
COUNTERS

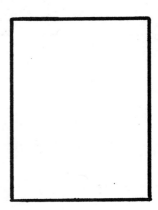

SHOW and COMPARE

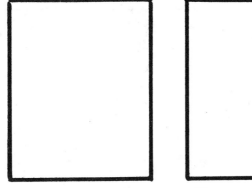

Place a number card here.

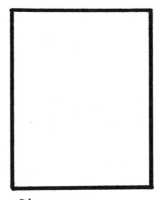

Place a >, <, or = card here.

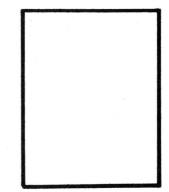

Place a number card here.

>	<	=	21	22	12
38	46	89	98	35	53

Teaching Aid 1.4

TRADING FRAME

Place trading cards here.

tens   ones

Trade 3 tens and 8ones for 2 tens and ___ ones.

Trade 7 tens and 2 ones for ___ tens and 12 ones.

Trade 5 tens and 16 ones for ___ tens and 6 ones.

Trade 2 tens and 13 ones for 3 tens and ___ ones.

Trade 8 tens and 11 ones for 9 tens and ___ ones.

Trade 1 group of 100 counters for 9 tens and ___ ones.

Fill in your own trading problem here.

Teaching Aid 1.5

From Exploring Mathematics: Activities for Concept and Skill Development, Copyright © 1990 Scott, Foresman and Company.

TOSS 'N' SHOW   Number Cubes Pattern

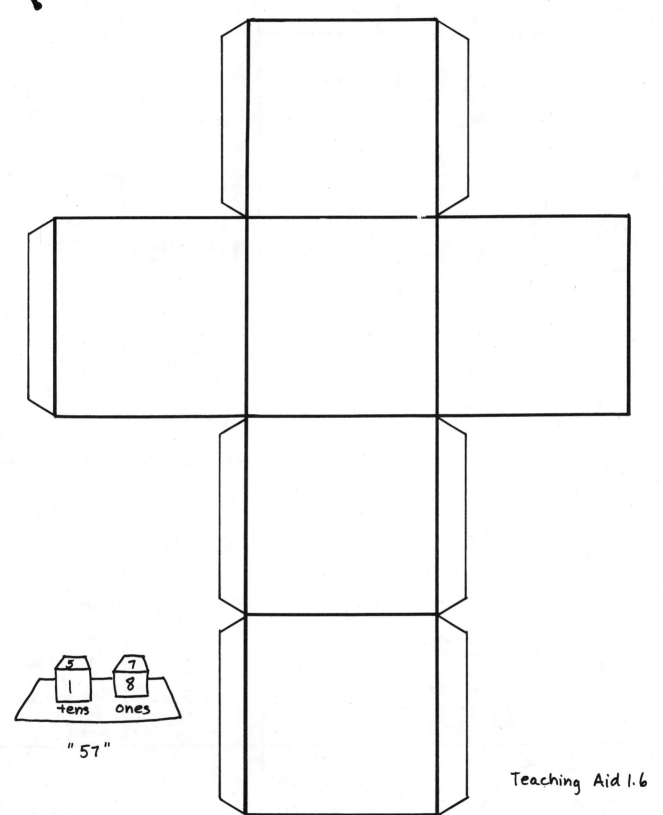

"57"

Teaching Aid 1.6

		1	●	one
△	2	⋮	△ △	two
3	●●●	△ △ △	three	4
●● ●●	△△△△	four	●● ●●●	5
△△ △△△	five	6	●●● ●●●	six
7	●●● ●●● ●	seven	8	△△△ △△△ △△
eight	9	●●● ●●● ●●●	△△△△ △△△△ △	nine

number cards for the

TREASURE HUNT

Teaching Aid 1.7b

		23	32	18
81	75	57	88	44
2 tens 8 ones	5 tens 3 ones	8 tens 7 ones	9 tens 2 ones	5 tens 5 ones
7 tens 4 ones	7 tens 1 one	4 tens	8 tens	7 ones
35	53	90	70	40
13	28	62	26	89
98	47	97	36	5

More Number - Numeral - Word Associations

MICE
and
BUNNIES

Teaching Aid
1.8a

More Number- Numeral -Word Associations

WORMS and Apples

Teaching Aid 1.8b

More Number- Numeral - Word Associations

RIDERS & HORSES

Teaching Aid 1.8c

2
Some Math Basics: Number Facts and Operations

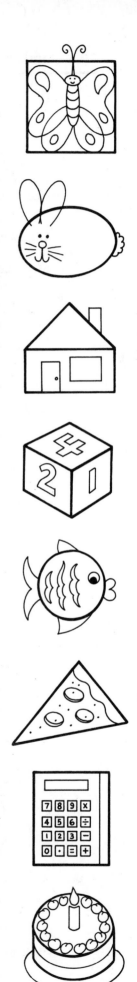

What is mathematics? Most people would immediately respond that math is computation and use of basic number facts. While computation is only a part of the entire scope of mathematics, it is a crucially important part. Children must understand what operations mean, and they must be able to give accurate answers to simple calculations. Building understanding takes time, appropriate activities, and opportunities to practice growing skills.

Before they deal with practicing basic facts and computations, children need developmental work on the meanings of operations. For instance, they must learn that subtraction is appropriate not only to "take-away" situations but also to making comparisons—e.g., "One set has how many more members than another?" Or, "How many more are needed?"

Children must start out by working with concrete manipulative materials to model operations. After they develop a conceptual base, they need regular drill on the facts of operations. Drill activities are best managed when done for short periods of time on a regular basis with plenty of encouragement.

A variety of activities will enhance the children's motivation to work on basic facts and operations. This chapter, therefore, offers that necessary variety to heighten children's motivation as they develop computational skills.

OVERHEAD FACTS

Small or large groups of children can use this handy, fast-paced activity for drill on basic facts.

Objective: Children will practice basic facts shown on the overhead projector.

Materials: Transparencies to copy Teaching Aids 2.1 and 2.2, stiff paper to reproduce number pointers (Teaching Aid 2.3), overhead projector, scissors.

Preparing for the Activity: Prepare the transparencies or draw similar ones to fit the facts your students are studying; prepare the pointers.

Approximate Time Frame: 20 minutes.

Conducting the Activity: To use Teaching Aid 2.1, let the children take turns coming up to the projector and using the pointers to show the answers to problems that you call out. Use problems like these: 8 + 7, show me 5 more than 7, 12 − 4, one less than 19.

For Teaching Aid 2.2, use basic multiplication facts such as these: 2 x 3, 5 x 2, and 4 x 3. You might also call out problems involving operations with tens—e.g., find 10 more than 32, point to 20 less than 38, show three groups of ten.

Evaluating the Activity: Did students find the correct answers quickly? Who seemed able to follow along saying the correct answers?

Extending the Activity: Let the children use Teaching Aid 2.1 or 2.2 by taking turns choosing an answer while their classmates tell one or more problems to go with the answer. If a child points to 12, for example, the problems might be 6 + 6, 18 − 6, 10 + 2, 3 x 4, and so on. Let small groups of children practice with the transparencies.

MEANINGS OF OPERATIONS

By working with concrete materials to represent arithmetic operations, children gain understanding of the meaning of the operations.

From *Exploring Mathematics: Activities for Concept and Skill Development*, Copyright © 1990 Scott, Foresman and Company.

Objectives: Children will use manipulatives to model computational operations and find answers.

Materials: Newspaper advertisements or catalog pages (possibly supplied by the children).

Preparing for the Activities: Choose the activities you want to use. Duplicate copies of the manipulatives (Teaching Aid 2.4a, b, c). Color and laminate the pieces, or have the children color them. You might also make a set of the manipulatives from felt or pellon for use on the flannel board.

Approximate Time Frame: Several sessions of 30 to 40 minutes each.

Conducting the Activities: Pose various problem situations and lead the children to arrange and count their manipulatives to solve the problems. Invite the children to create similar problems for their classmates to solve. Record appropriate number sentences on the chalkboard as the children work. From time to time, have the children record number sentences for the situations they represent with their manipulatives.

Here are some problem situations you can pose for various arithmetic operations:

Addition. Addition is the union of disjoint sets. Represent situations such as "I have two apples, then get four more. How many apples do I have in all?" "Tom has three hats. Josie has five hats. How many hats do they have together?"

Let the children work in groups of four or five to lay out pieces representing what they might eat for lunch. Ask: "How many sandwiches did your group have altogether? How many drinks are here?" Ask the children to hold two pieces of fruit in their left hands and three pieces in their right hands. See if they can tell how many pieces of fruit they have in all without actually moving their hands together.

Subtraction. Subtraction has three interpretations: take-away, comparison, and how many more are needed. Children need a great deal of experience with all three interpretations.

The take-away interpretation is easy to understand. Have children arrange some manipulatives, take some away, and see how many are left. For example, "Kenny had five hot dogs. He gave three away. How many hot dogs did Kenny have left?"

For the comparison interpretation, have the children arrange two sets side by side. For instance, "Here are Anna's six hats. Here are Kevin's four hats. Who has more hats? How many more?" The children will see that four hats have "partners," but three (the answer to how many more) do not have "partners."

The how many more are needed (or missing addend) interpretation can be easily illustrated with manipulatives. Use a situation such as "Alice needs eight apples for a party snack. She has three apples. How many more apples should she buy?" Have the children first arrange three apples, and then add more apples until they have eight. They thus learn that Alice needs to buy five more apples.

Multiplication. Some interpretations of multiplication include equivalent sets or repeated addition, skip counting, arrays or rectangular arrangements, and Cartesian products. Use problems such as "Jody eats two apples a day for seven days. How many apples does he eat in all?" Have the children arrange pictures to represent the apples. Encourage skip counting of the apples—2, 4, 6, 8, 10, 12, 14. Use other examples of repeated addition, solving them by regular and skip counting.

To illustrate arrays, have the children work in groups and neatly arrange the face pictures. Say to them: "Make four rows with two faces in each row. How many faces did you use?" You might also have the children use squared paper to cut out various rectangles (e.g., 5 by 3 squares or 7 by 8 squares) and then find the total number of squares.

Finally, use the Cartesian products interpretation which involves matching every member of one set with every member of a second set. For example, ask the students: "If you had three different kinds of sandwiches and two kinds of drinks, how many different combinations of one sandwich and one drink could you make?" "Use two faces and eight hats. How many different ways can you arrange them?"

Evaluating the Activities: Watch the children as they work. Determine who works confidently and correctly. See which children appear to be leaders in the activities.

Extending the Activities: Mix the operations in the problems you present. Introduce multi-digit problems for the children to work on in groups.

FACT PRACTICE PALS

Children love to use the self-checking activity suggested here to practice their basic facts. By permitting problems to be personalized for each child's needs, this activity provides individualized practice.

Objective: Children will practice basic facts using a self-checking format.

Materials: Paper to reproduce at least one practice pal (Teaching Aid 2.5a or b) per child, crayons, scissors.

Preparing for the Activity: Work with the children to determine which facts they need to practice. You might use a timed test and have the children

From *Exploring Mathematics: Activities for Concept and Skill Development,* Copyright © 1990 Scott, Foresman and Company.

note which facts they miss. You also might let the children try to identify "shaky" facts themselves. For example, one child might know that she needs practice on all the 17s, 18s, and 19s in subtraction. Another child might be aware that he needs to practice multiplication facts with sixes.

Duplicate a practice pal for each child. Let each child color the figure, cut it out, and cut out the question-answer slit as shown on the pattern. Show the children how to write facts and answers on the figures' "tongues." Children can use counters or operation tables to find the answers to the problems they need to practice.

Approximate Time Frame: 30 minutes to prepare materials, 10 to 15 minutes practice time on subsequent days.

Conducting the Activity: Set aside a short period of time each day for the children to use their fact Practice Pals. Show them how to pull out the tongue to reveal the first problem. After they say or write the answer, have them pull out the tongue a little further to reveal the answer. If a child misses the answer, he or she should look at, say, and write the *entire problem.*

As the children become familiar with using their Practice Pals, they can make longer tongues from paper strips or adding machine paper. After mastering some facts, they can add others on different tongues.

Evaluating the Activity: Observe the children as they work, noting who stays on task and who assumes responsibility for working on needed facts. Retest the children periodically to formally assess their progress in mastering basic facts.

Extending the Activity: Use pictures of small clocks or coins on the tongues. You can also have either geometric shapes with their names or numerals with their number names on the tongues. Allow children who know their facts to use Practice Pals to tutor children who need help. Encourage each child to keep track of his or her own progress, perhaps noting during each practice session the number of facts tried and the number of facts correctly answered.

NUMBER SCAVENGER HUNTS

Add a light and unusual touch to computation practice by having the children search for numbers and then use the numbers in computations.

Objectives: Children will find and record specified numbers. They will use the numbers in addition, subtraction, multiplication, and division problems.

Materials: Paper to reproduce scavenger hunt lists (Teaching Aid 2.6a and b) and awards (Teaching Aid 2.6b), newspaper pages with lots of numerals (all pages need not be the same), scissors.

Preparing for the Activities: Duplicate one or more of the lists for each child or each small group of children. Provide newspaper ad pages for the children to use in their number scavenger hunts. Select a scavenger hunt that suits your students' needs. Duplicate the awards.

Approximate Time Frame: 20 minutes per scavenger hunt.

Conducting the Activities: Hand out the scavenger hunt lists for the type of hunt you choose. If the children are to look for numerals in the newspaper, have them show you some examples of the kinds of numbers they will be looking for before they begin the hunt. If the children are to look at home for numbers on can and box labels, show a few examples; be sure to point out where to look on the packages for the numbers.

Review the scavenger lists with the children, and give them enough time to complete the hunt. Spot-check answers, but also encourage the children to check each other and to share and compare answers.

Evaluating the Activities: Observe the children and see who works quietly and cooperatively. Spot-check the children's answers to make certain that they are doing their work correctly.

Extending the Activity: Invite the children to suggest other kinds of activities they could use for a computation scavenger hunt. Have groups of children compile scavenger hunt lists for their classmates to use. Conduct a scavenger hunt for geometric shapes.

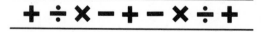

FLASH CARD PROFUSION

Practice with flash cards helps many youngsters learn their basic facts. Because a choice of flash card formats is often motivating, you may want to present many kinds of flash cards and let students selects the ones they like best.

From *Exploring Mathematics: Activities for Concept and Skill Development,* Copyright © 1990 Scott, Foresman and Company.

Objectives: Children will make flash cards and use them to practice basic facts.

Materials: Construction paper or file folders to reproduce flash cards (Teaching Aid 2.7a, b, c), paper to reproduce children's record sheet (Teaching Aid 2.7c), boxes to store flash cards (possibly supplied by the children), scissors, crayons, markers, hole punch, glue.

Preparing for the Activity: Pretest the children to determine which basic facts they need to learn. Present several flash card formats to the children, showing them how to use each one. Let each child select a kind of flash card to work with and make cards for the facts he or she needs to practice.

For the Fact Sandwiches, have children write fact "families" on the sandwich pieces. For example, a child might use $8 + 6$, $7 + 7$, $9 + 5$, $13 + 1$, $10 + 4$, $14 - 8$, $14 - 7$, $14 - 5$, and $14 - 1$ as sandwich pieces for the "14 family." Each child should prepare two or more families and write the answers on the backs. Then the child shuffles the pieces, groups the families back together, and checks the answers. Work with the sandwiches gives children practice in both horizontal and vertical presentation of facts.

You might let each child decorate a small box and make two dividers for the box: "Facts I Know" and "Facts I Need to Practice." The children can use their boxes for card storage after each practice session.

Approximate Time Frame: 30 minutes to prepare the cards; 10 to 15 minutes of practice time on subsequent days.

Conducting the Activity: Let the children work in pairs, using their cards to present basic facts to each other and checking one another. Encourage the pairs to talk in low voices. When a child misses a fact, he or she should check the answer and then say the *entire problem* to him- or herself. Some children find it helpful to trace over the numerals of problems they have missed while saying the problem aloud.

Encourage the children to keep track of their progress each time they practice, perhaps marking forms such as the ones in Teaching Aid 2.7c. Emphasize that progress in learning the facts is an individual task; each student can master the facts, but some require more work with the flash cards—and other kinds of practice—than others do.

Evaluating the Activity: Check the children's records of their progress. After a suitable number of practice sessions, administer a timed test of appropriate basic facts.

Extending the Activity: Let children make and use their own designs for flash cards.

$$\div \times - + - \times \div$$

CHAPTER

2

TEACHING

AIDS

$$\div \times - + - \times \div$$

10   9   2

17   11

0

12   19   6

5

16

7   13

18   3

15   1

14   20

4   8

Teaching Aid 2.1   Transparency Master   Numbers 0-20

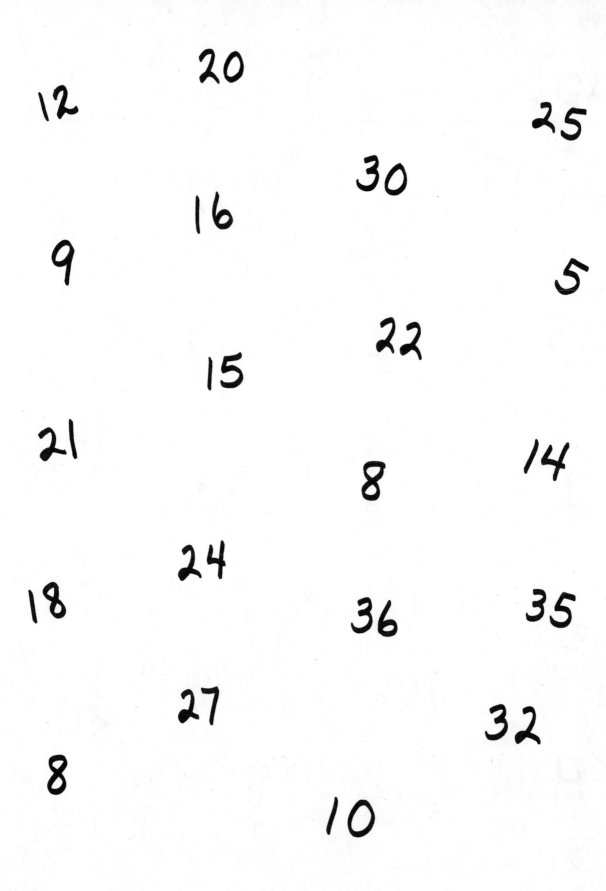

12   20   25

        30

    16

9   5

        22

    15

21   14

        8

    24

18   35

    27   32

8

        10

Teaching Aid 2.2   Easy Multiplication Facts

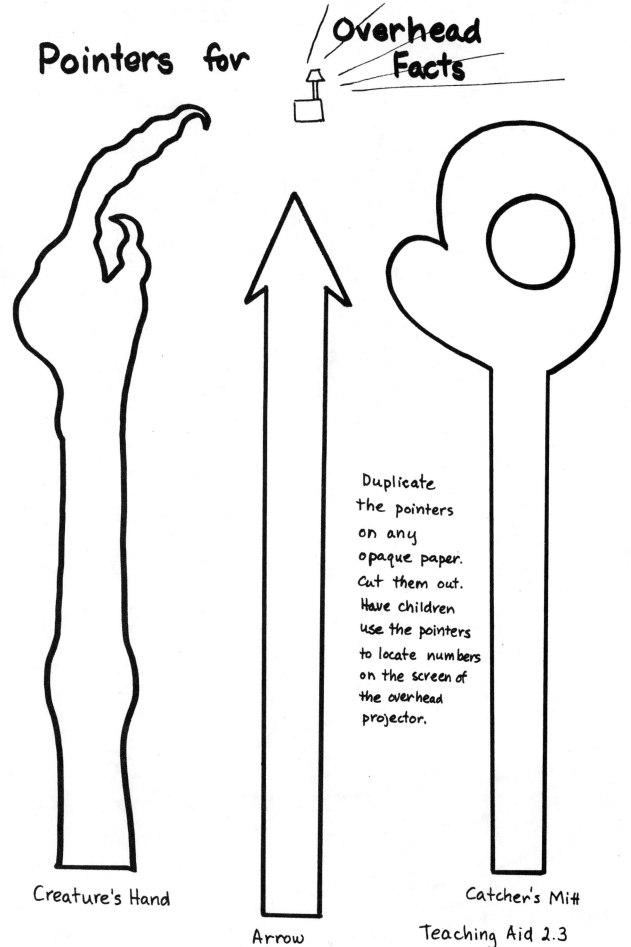

Pointers for Overhead Facts

Creature's Hand

Arrow

Duplicate the pointers on any opaque paper. Cut them out. Have children use the pointers to locate numbers on the screen of the overhead projector.

Catcher's Mitt

Teaching Aid 2.3

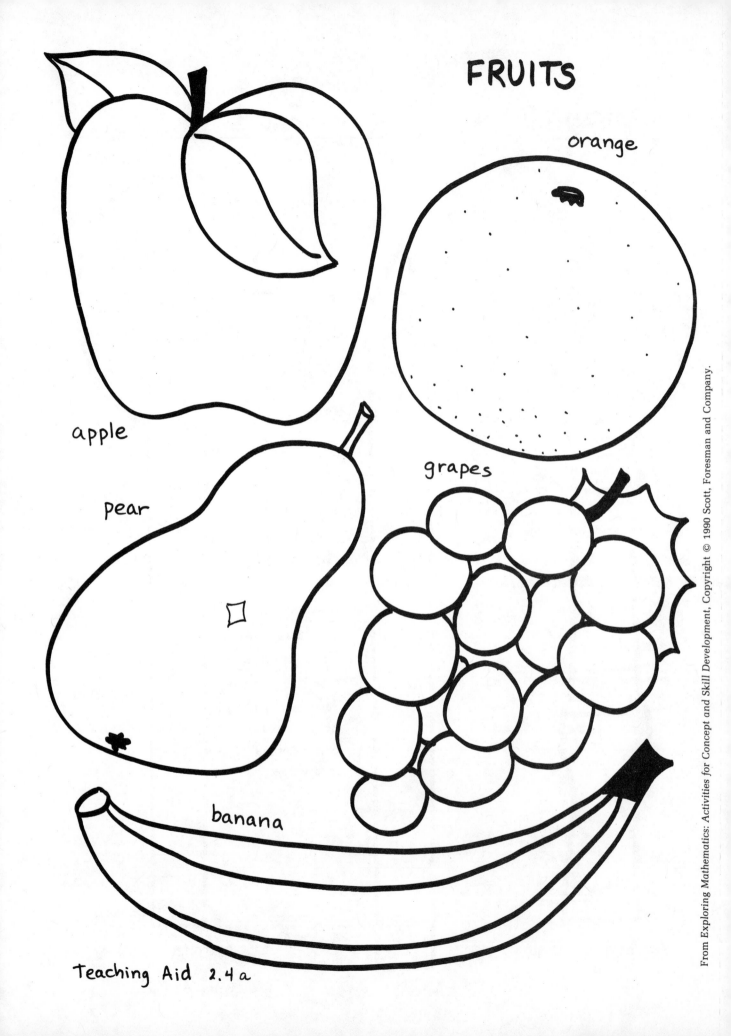

FRUITS

orange

apple

pear

grapes

banana

Teaching Aid 2.4a

From Exploring Mathematics: Activities for Concept and Skill Development, Copyright © 1990 Scott, Foresman and Company.

HATS AND FACES

Teaching Aid 2.4b

SANDWICHES AND DRINKS

milk

soda

peanut butter
sandwich

hamburger

hot dog

RÖBÖT Practice Pal

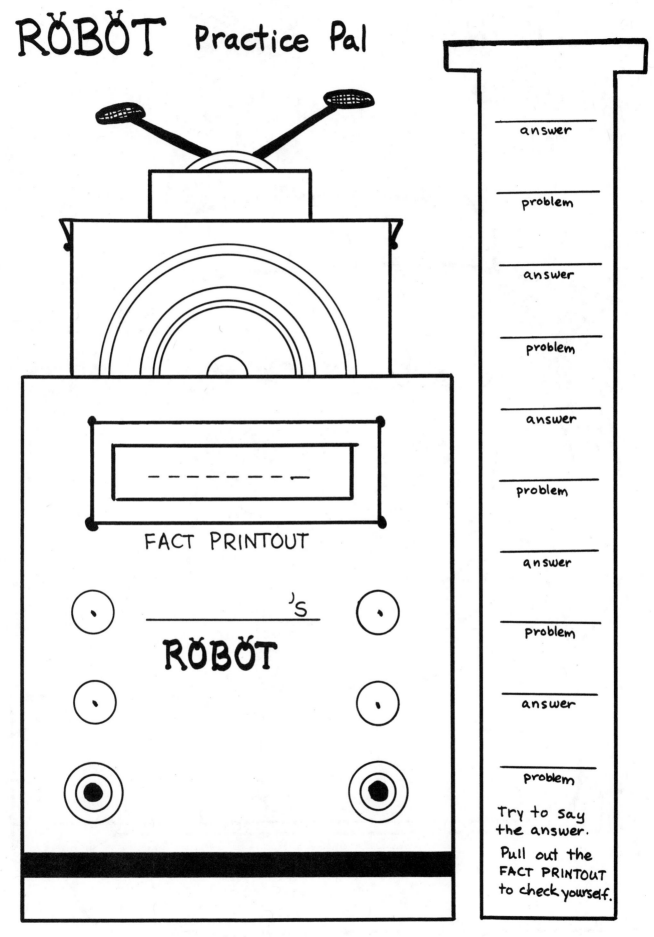

answer

problem

answer

problem

answer

problem

answer

problem

answer

problem

FACT PRINTOUT

_____'s

RÖBÖT

Try to say the answer.

Pull out the FACT PRINTOUT to check yourself.

Teaching Aid 2.5 a

CLOWN
Practice
Pal

My Special Numbers
SCAVENGER HUNT

Write your special numbers below

- Street, apartment, or box number _____
- Your age _____
- A family member's age _____
- Your telephone number _____

Put the numbers in order -- from smallest to largest

_____ _____ _____ _____

Write the total of the numbers. _____

Write the difference of the largest and smallest numbers. _____

---

the Great  Scavenger Hunt

Look at the license plates on cars and other vehicles.

- Sketch a license plate where the sum of its numbers is 10.

- Find a license plate where all the numbers are odd.

- Sketch any license plate. Find the difference in the sum of the odd numbers and even numbers on the plate.

- Sketch a plate where a multiple of 6 occurs anywhere in the number.

 Scavenger Hunt

- Find 3 numbers greater than 80 but less than 120. Write them here. Find their sum.

  _____ + _____ + _____ =

- Find 3 numbers with a sum of 12. Tape them here.

  _____ + _____ + _____ _____

- Find 3 numbers that can be evenly divided by 4. Tape them here.

  _____ _____ _____

- Tape a number less than 200 here. Multiply the number by 3. Write the answer. _____

KITCHEN CABINET Scavenger Hunt

Find and record numbers you find in your kitchen cabinets or pantry.

- Number of grams in a can of soup. _____
- Number of grams in a can of fruit or vegetables. _____
- Length of something sold by length. _____
- Find something sold by volume. Record its volume. _____

Add all the numbers above. Subtract the total from 10000. Double the total.

Number Scavenger Hunts Task Cards   Teaching Aid 2.6a

NEWSPAPER  SCAVENGER HUNT

Cut out the numbers 1-9.
Glue each in its box.

four	five	eight
six	nine	two
one	three	seven

Cut out
at least
5 fives.

Glue
them on
the big
numeral 5.

5

Glue the answer to each in the box.

2+4 = ☐   7+3 = ☐   4+2+5 = ☐

Awards
for
Number Scavenger
Hunts

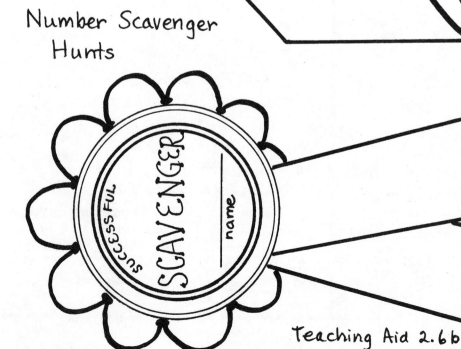

I completed a
NUMBER
SCAVENGER
HUNT

name ___

SUCCESSFUL SCAVENGER

name ___

Teaching Aid 2.6b

From Exploring Mathematics: Activities for Concept and Skill Development, Copyright © 1990 Scott, Foresman and Company.

FLASH CARD   PROFUSION

Triangular Cards

Write addition facts on the cards, putting the sum on top. Do not use signs. Or write multiplication facts.

Use the cards to practice both addition and subtraction. To add, hold a pack of cards and cover the sum.

To subtract, cover a bottom number.

Cover-Up Cards

Write a complete fact on the card filling in all the blanks. Cut out and fold the cover-up strip below. Glue it together. Slip the strip over one part of the fact. Say the answer. Move the strip to check.

problem 2+☐=6   2+4=☐ check

Glue here

FACT SANDWICHES

peanut butter

catsup, mustard, or mayonnaise

bread

hamburger

bun

cheese

lettuce

lunch meat

From Exploring Mathematics: Activities for Concept and Skill Development, Copyright © 1990 Scott, Foresman and Company.

Teaching Aid 2.7b

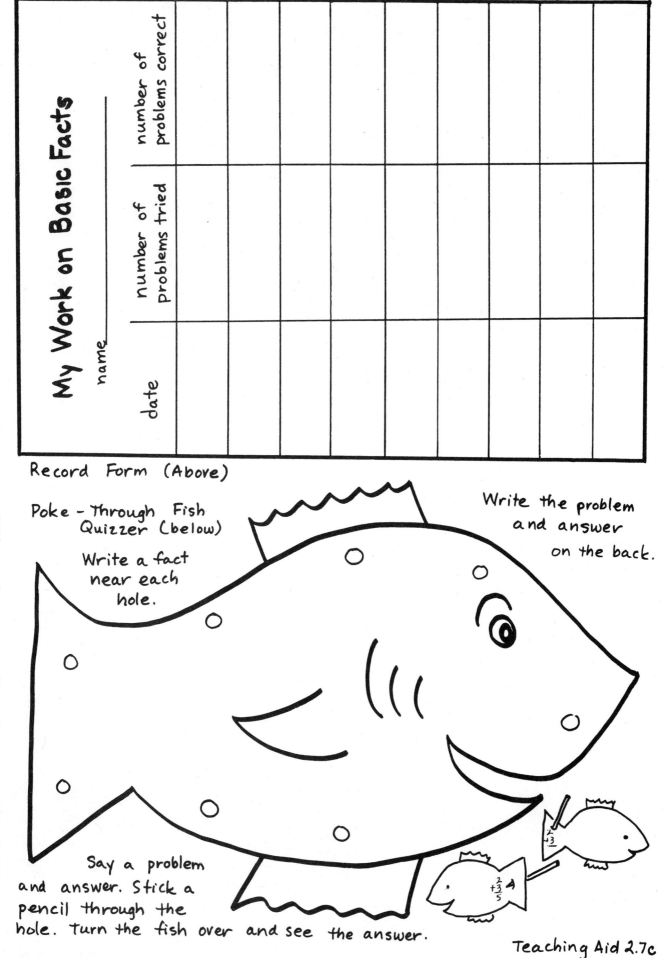

My Work on Basic Facts

name _____

date	number of problems tried	number of problems correct

Record Form (Above)

Poke – Through Fish
Quizzer (below)

Write a fact
near each
hole.

Write the problem
and answer
on the back.

Say a problem
and answer. Stick a
pencil through the
hole. Turn the fish over and see the answer.

Teaching Aid 2.7c

3

Now Let Me Think...
Problem Solving

People are involved in problem solving throughout their lives. For young children, problem solving might involve dealing with physical objects, working with numerical situations, or encountering geometric-spatial relationships.

When a child knows immediately what to do in a situation, the situation really has not presented a problem. Problem solving, therefore, involves thinking, reasoning, and application of skills. To do it well takes time, thought, effort, and checking.

George Polya, famous for his work on the problem-solving process, suggested four steps for problem solving:

1. Understand the problem. See what you are to do and what you have to "go on."
2. Develop a plan to solve the problem. This step is creative; it involves decision-making.
3. Carry out the plan. Do the work as planned.
4. Look back and evaluate the solution. Check yourself. If the solution is incorrect, try again, starting over with step 1 or 2.

Even young children can apply these steps as they work with puzzling situations and non-routine problems.

The problems presented in this chapter are varied. Many have several good answers, a situation that occurs often in life. Some of the problems involve computation; others involve work with and rearrangement of objects. Children may work on the problems independently, but small group work is also recommended—problem solving often is a process in which "several heads are better than one."

Have the children practice problem solving frequently. In addition to using the problems in this chapter as they are presented here, you can place them in a special "puzzle center" or put them up on a bulletin board as your "Problem of the Day" (or week).

Because there are alternative approaches to working most problems, make a practice of letting children share their solutions and problem-solving strategies. Reward solutions, but also encourage "sticking with" problems—effort and persistence are characteristics of good problem solvers.

PUZZLE CORNER

Encourage problem solving by building up interest in a puzzle corner—a special place where children can voluntarily try a variety of problems.

Objective: Children will attempt to solve a variety of problems.

Materials: Paper to reproduce puzzle cards and awards from Teaching Aid 3.1, materials to create a bulletin board or puzzle center, scissors.

Preparing for the Activity: Fix a special area of the room for a puzzle corner or problem-solving niche. Some suggestions for arranging such an area are found in Teaching Aid 3.1a. Duplicate the task cards (Teaching Aids 3.1b, d, e, f) and the sorting pieces (Teaching Aid 3.1c). Display the task cards just one or two at a time, but change them once or twice a week. Duplicate some problem-solving awards.

You might duplicate the answers (found in Teaching Aid 3.2 due to their length) and tape them to the backs of the math puzzle task cards.

Approximate Time Frame: 10 to 20 minutes, depending on the problems.

Conducting the Activity: Introduce the problem-solving center to the children and outline some ground rules for its use. The rules you set will be pertinent to your own teaching situation, but here are some general guidelines you should consider:

Work in the center one or two at a time.

Use your own paper.

Do your own work.

Check your answers with the teacher. If you solve a problem, you may sign your name to the "I Solved It" list.

Keep answers secret! Each person must have the opportunity to solve the problems independently.

Bring contributions for the puzzle corner as often as you wish.

After as many children who want an opportunity have had their chance to solve the current "Puzzle Corner" problem, discuss their strategies for working on the problem as well as their answers to it.

Evaluating the Activity: Note the children's interest, persistence, and ability to solve problems. You might want to write the answers on the backs of puzzle cards and have the children—only after they are satisfied that they have completed work on the problems—use the honor system to check themselves.

Extending the Activity: Use problems that the children contribute in the puzzle corner. Add these problems to your own collection of appropriate problems.

From *Exploring Mathematics: Activities for Concept and Skill Development,* Copyright © 1990 Scott, Foresman and Company.

LET'S GO SHOPPING

People of all ages love to shop. The following activity presents children with lots of shopping choices as they apply problem-solving skills.

Objective: Children will apply computational skills as they solve shopping problems.

Materials: Paper to duplicate task cards from Teaching Aid 3.3a, b, c, old catalogs or newspaper ads (possibly supplied by the children), scissors, tape or glue.

Preparing for the Activity: Duplicate one or more of the task cards. Also duplicate some "Funny Money" from Teaching Aid 3.6 for "Shopping for Little Things."

Approximate Time Frame: 20 minutes per task.

Conducting the Activity: Instruct the children to browse through the ads or catalogs and select items they would like to buy. Show them how to cut out pictures of items—or the phrases that describe the items—and how to attach the pictures or phrases to their papers with tape or glue. Since the children's papers will vary, ask them to check one another's completed solutions mentally, using pencil and paper, or with a calculator. Lead the children in a discussion of why they made the choices they did.

Evaluating the Activity: Spot-check the children's papers.

Extending the Activity: Invite the children to make shopping problems for each other. Have them "shop" for seasonal items, compare sale prices to regular prices, and discuss what makes a bargain.

STICKS AND STONES

These problems involve spatial reasoning and some unconventional thinking. Since the children manipulate real objects to find the solutions, however, the problem-solving process is very concrete.

Objectives: Children will manipulate objects and try to solve spatial-reasoning problems.

Materials: Paper to duplicate task cards from Teaching Aid 3.4a, b, c, d, toothpicks or straws, small round objects.

Preparing for the Activity: Duplicate copies of the task cards for each small group of children or for your problem-solving center. Give each group about 20 toothpicks or straws and 15 small round objects (stones, pennies, round counters, or round Styrofoam bits).

Approximate Time Frame: 30 minutes.

Conducting the Activity: Tell the children that they will be working with long markers ("sticks") and round markers ("stones") for these problem-solving activities. Have the children work in small groups, following the directions and manipulating their sticks and stones to solve the problems.

   If many of the children get "stuck" on problem 2, offer the clue that the squares need not be of the same size. Allow plenty of time for solutions. Have the children share their solutions.

   Here are the answers to the problems presented on the task cards.

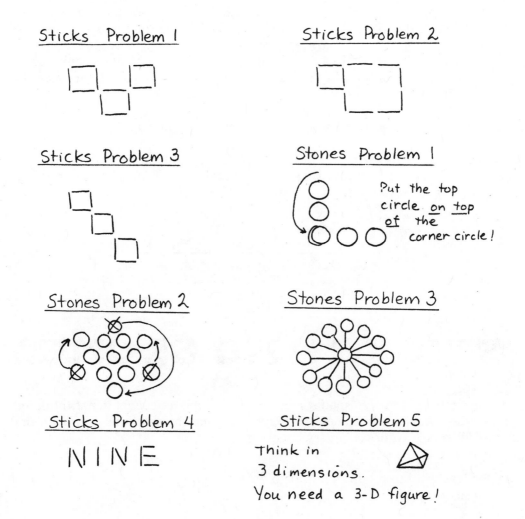

From *Exploring Mathematics: Activities for Concept and Skill Development*, Copyright © 1990 Scott, Foresman and Company.

Evaluating the Activity: Note whether the children work cooperatively and employ several different strategies as they work. See who sticks with the problems until finding solutions.

Extending the Activity: Ask the children to share the problems with their families and to discuss their results with the class. Invite the children to create and share similar problems with the class.

+ ÷ ✕ − + − ✕ ÷ +

MONEY PUZZLERS

Each of these money problems has more than one solution. Children can generate, check, and compare their answers.

Objective: Children will suggest combinations of coins to yield given values.

Materials: Paper to reproduce worksheets from Teaching Aid 3.5a or b, real or pretend coins, or "Funny Money" from Teaching Aid 3.6.

Preparing for the Activity: Duplicate the worksheets and gather the money.

Approximate Time Frame: 30 minutes for each worksheet.

Conducting the Activity: For Teaching Aid 3.5a, ask the children to suggest several combinations of coins to make 37 cents. Let the children take turns selecting and counting out coins to make the 37 cents total, starting with the largest coins. Show them how to record the number of coins they used. Next, use the worksheet for independent work or work with partners. Let the children verify and share their answers in groups of six to eight or with the entire class.

For Teaching Aid 3.5b, emphasize to the children that the number of coins they can use is limited. Try the problem using four coins to make 40 cents (possible answers include 10 + 10 + 10 + 10 and 25 + 5 + 5 + 5). Show the children how to work with the coins or with pencil and paper to check solutions to the problems on the worksheet. After a work session, have the children share their answers in small groups or with the entire class.

The list below presents several answers for the problems presented on Teaching Aid 3.5b. Check other answers the children offer.

1. 5 dimes
   1 quarter, 1 dime, 3 nickels

2. 1 half dollar, 1 dime, 3 nickels
   2 quarters, 2 dimes, 1 nickel

3. 1 quarter, 3 dimes, 4 nickels
   1 half dollar, 2 dimes, 5 pennies

4. 9 dimes, 2 nickels
   1 half dollar, 4 dimes, 1 nickel, 5 pennies

5. Problems and answers will vary.

Evaluating the Activity: Notice the ease with which children count coins and associate coins with their values. See which children check their own work without being prompted. For children who need extra help, provide a learning center with coins to count, compare, and match with cards that specify values.

Extending the Activity: Use different numbers for similar problems. Ask the children to notice change being counted in stores and restaurants. Use problems that the children suggest with the entire class.

From *Exploring Mathematics: Activities for Concept and Skill Development*, Copyright © 1990 Scott, Foresman and Company.

÷ ✕ − ✚ − ✕ ÷

CHAPTER

3

TEACHING

AIDS

÷ ✕ − ✚ − ✕ ÷

PUZZLE CORNER

Make a mini-puzzle carrel inside a box.

A bulletin board and table space makes a puzzle corner.

Screens made from cardboard make 4 carrels for a table-top puzzle center. You could also use the screens on the floor.

PROBLEM SOLVING CERTIFICATE

Awarded To

_____

For ability in problem solving

* persistence
* creativity
* application of math skills

Teaching Aid 3.1a

SORTING FUN #1

Sort the pictures into 2 piles. Make 1 pile for objects that <u>fasten</u> things together. Make the other pile for objects that <u>don't</u> <u>fasten</u> things together.

SORTING FUN #2

Sort the pictures into 2 piles. Make 1 pile for things used <u>for drawing, painting, or writing.</u> Make the other pile for things <u>not</u> used for <u>drawing, painting, or writing.</u>

SORTING FUN #3

Sort the pictures into 2 piles. Make 1 pile for things used <u>for eating.</u> Make the other pile for things <u>not used for eating.</u>

SORTING FUN #4

Sort the pictures into 2 or more piles. <u>Decide</u> for yourself how you will sort them. Let a friend check you.

Sorting Fun Task Cards   Puzzle Corner   Teaching Aid 3.1b

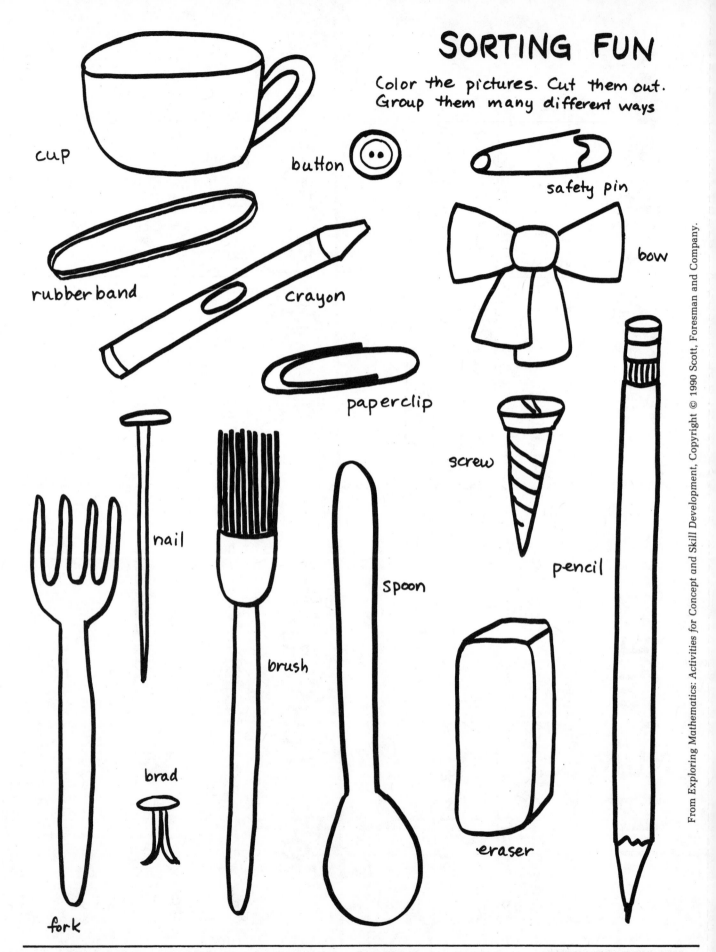

SORTING FUN

Color the pictures. Cut them out.
Group them many different ways

cup

button

safety pin

rubber band

crayon

bow

paperclip

screw

nail

brush

spoon

pencil

fork

brad

eraser

SAME
U
M
S

Cut out the circles from the bottom row.

Arrange the cut-out circles on the triangular arrangement so that the sum on each side of the triangle is the same.

There are two ways to do this problem. Can you find them both?

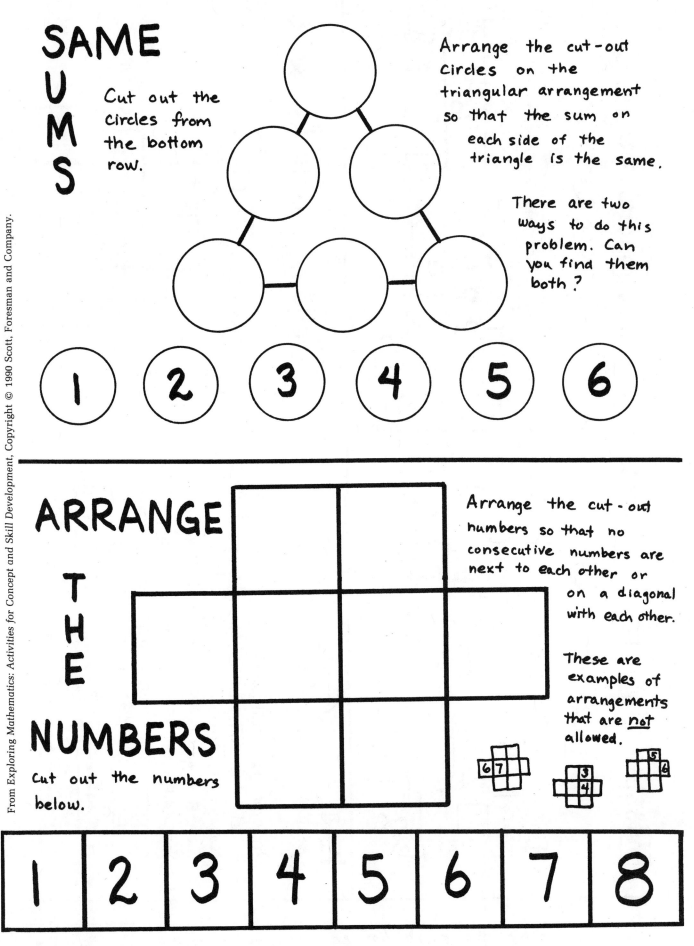

ARRANGE
T
H
E
NUMBERS

Cut out the numbers below.

Arrange the cut-out numbers so that no consecutive numbers are next to each other or on a diagonal with each other.

These are examples of arrangements that are not allowed.

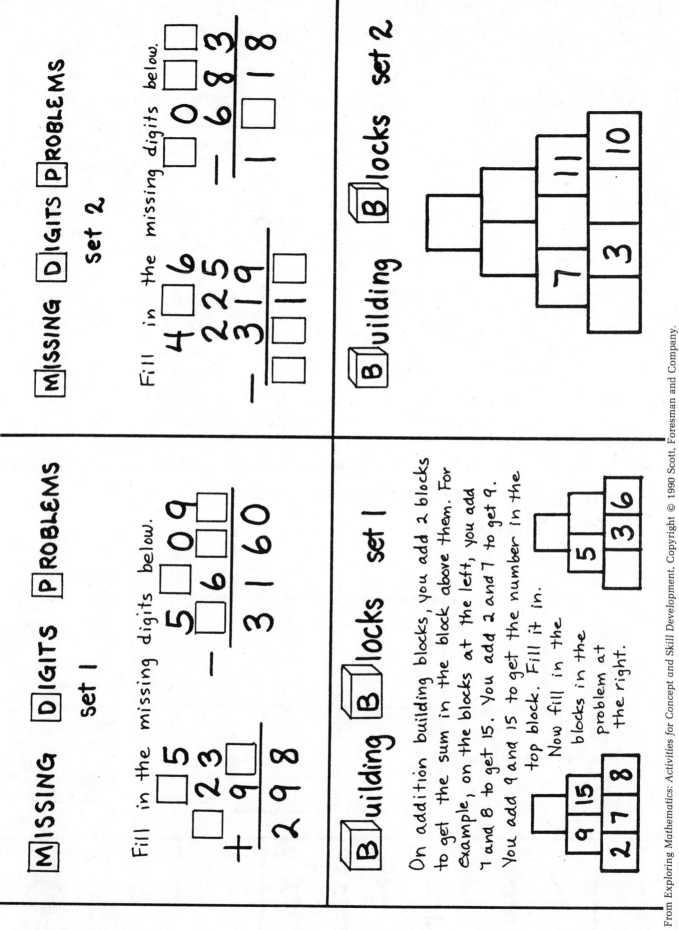

Missing Digits Problems — set 1

Fill in the missing digits below.

```
   □ 5
   2 3
 + □
 ─────
   2 9 8
```

```
   5 □ 9
 - □ 6
 ─────
   3 6 0
```

Missing Digits Problems — set 2

Fill in the missing digits below.

```
   4 □ 6
   2 2 5
   3 □ 9
 + □ □ □
 ─────────
   □ □ □
```

```
   □ □ 0
 - 6 8 3
 ─────
   1 □ 8
```

Building Blocks — set 1

On addition building blocks, you add 2 blocks to get the sum in the block above them. For example, on the blocks at the left, you add 7 and 8 to get 15. You add 2 and 8 to get 15. You add 2 and 7 to get 9. You add 9 and 15 to get the number in the top block. Fill it in.

Now fill in the blocks in the problem at the right.

```
   9 | 15
   2 | 7 | 8
```

```
     | 5 |
   3 | 6 |
```

Building Blocks — set 2

```
     |    |
   7 | 11 |
     | 3 | 10
```

🅱️uilding 🅱️locks set 4

Fill in the blanks on the building blocks problem.

This building blocks problem uses multiplication.
You multiply 2 blocks to get the number in the block above them.

```
[  ]
[10][15]
[ 2][  ][ 3]
```

🅱️uilding 🅱️locks set 3

Fill in the missing numbers on this addition building blocks problem.

```
[  ]
[  ][14]
[10][ 8][ 3]
```

FILL IN THE PATTERN set 2

Study the number patterns. Try to fill in the missing numbers. Check yourself with the numbers that are given.

1, 3, 7, 15, ___, ___, 127, ___,

0, 1, 8, ___, ___, 125, ___,

1, 1, 2, 3, 5, 8, ___, ___, 34,

FILL IN THE PATTERN set 1

Study the number patterns. Try to fill in the missing numbers. Check yourself with the numbers that are given.

0, 1, 3, 6, 10, ___, ___, 28, ___

50, 43, 44, 37, 38, ___, ___, 25, ___

2, 4, 3, 6, ___, 10, ___, ___, 17, ___

Same Sums

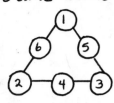

Each sum is 9.

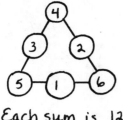

Each sum is 12.

Arrange the Numbers

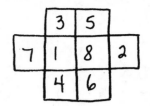

Missing Digits   set 1

$$\begin{array}{r} 85 \\ 123 \\ +\ 90 \\ \hline 298 \end{array}$$

$$\begin{array}{r} 5809 \\ -2649 \\ \hline 3160 \end{array}$$

Missing Digits   set 2

$$\begin{array}{r} 466 \\ 225 \\ +\ 319 \\ \hline 1010 \end{array}$$

$$\begin{array}{r} 2001 \\ -\ 683 \\ \hline 1318 \end{array}$$

Building Blocks   set 1

Building Blocks   set 2

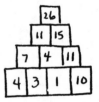

Building Blocks   set 3

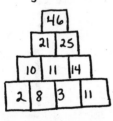

Building Blocks   set 4

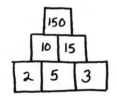

Fill in the Pattern   set 1

0, 1, 3, 6, 10, <u>15</u>, <u>21</u>, 28, <u>36</u>

50, 43, 44, 37, 38, <u>31</u>, <u>32</u>, 25, <u>26</u>

2, 4, 3, 6, <u>5</u>, 10, <u>9</u>, 18, 17, 34

Fill in the Pattern   set 2

1, 3, 7, 15, <u>31</u>, <u>63</u>, 127, <u>255</u>, <u>511</u>

0, 1, 8, <u>27</u>, <u>64</u>, 125, <u>216</u>

1, 1, 2, 3, 5, 8, <u>13</u>, <u>21</u>, 34, <u>55</u>

Sort the Pictures -- Answers will vary.

Answers for the Puzzle Corner   Teaching Aid 3.2

From *Exploring Mathematics: Activities for Concept and Skill Development*, Copyright © 1990 Scott, Foresman and Company.

LET'S EAT!

Use a grocery ad and select things you would buy.
Make choices for the following list. You have a $20 limit.
Cut out prices and pictures of the items you select.
Tape them to the list. Find your total. Figure your change.

Something to drink   a bread

a fruit   a meat   a snack

DRESS YOURSELF

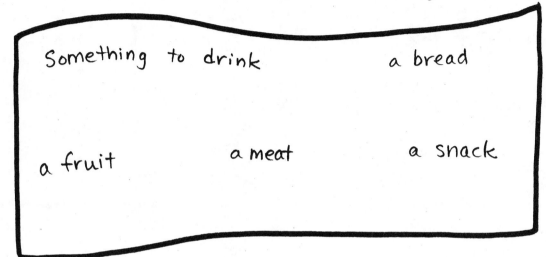

Use clothing ads or a catalog. Shop for a
complete outfit for yourself for under $100.00.
Cut out pictures of what you will buy. Tape
them here. Figure your total and change.

LUNCH FOR TWO

Use a grocery ad. Choose what you would buy for lunch for yourself and a friend. Tape prices and pictures below. Show your prices and totals on the list.

PRICES

TOTAL

FOOTWEAR

Use a catalog or newspaper ad. Find prices for these things:
- 2 pairs socks   3 pairs shoes
- 1 pair boots

Tape the prices to the foot picture. Is your total greater than or less than $200.00?

By how much?

_____

From Exploring Mathematics: Activities for Concept and Skill Development, Copyright © 1990 Scott, Foresman and Company.

Shopping for LITTLE THINGS

Find 3 things that cost less than $1.00. Tape them below.
Place coins on each to
show the prices.

SHOPPING FUN

Find pictures of things that cost less than $10.00. Tape them below. Find the total of both prices.

SCRAMBLED
Sticks Problem 1

Arrange 17 toothpicks like the picture.
Now <u>remove 5 toothpicks</u> and <u>leave 3 squares.</u>

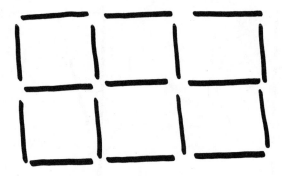

SCRAMBLED
Sticks Problem 2

Arrange 17 toothpicks like this. Now
<u>remove 6 toothpicks</u> and <u>leave</u> just <u>2 squares.</u>

From Exploring Mathematics: Activities for Concept and Skill Development, Copyright © 1990 Scott, Foresman and Company.

SCRAMBLED
Sticks Problem 3

Arrange 12 toothpicks like the picture.

Rearrange 4 toothpicks to leave 3 squares.

Arrange 6 stones -- pennies
or styrofoam circles -- like
the picture. Make 4 circles
vertically. (Up and down)
Make 3 circles horizontally.
(Across)

Move just 1 circle to make
4 circles in each row --
horizontally and vertically.

Problem 2

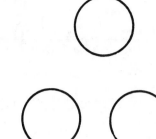

Arrange 10 stones -- styrofoam circles or pennies -- like the picture.

Now rearrange just 3 stones so that you have a new triangular arrangement that points in the opposite direction -- like this:

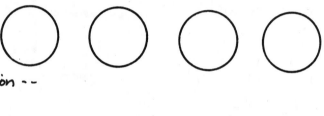

Problem 3

For this problem use 13 stones -- pennies or styrofoam circles.

Arrange them in 6 lines with 3 stones in each line.

Sticks 'N' Stones   Problem Cards

Teaching Aid 3.4c

From Exploring Mathematics: Activities for Concept and Skill Development, Copyright © 1990 Scott, Foresman and Company.

SCRAMBLED
Sticks Problem 4

When does 5+6 make 9? Let's find out.
Arrange 6 toothpicks like this.

| | | | | |

Now add 5 more toothpicks to make nine.

SCRAMBLED
Sticks Problem 5

An equilateral triangle is the same length
on each side. It looks like this. △

Use 6 toothpicks. From the toothpicks, make
4 equilateral triangles, all the same size.

MANY COIN COMBINATIONS

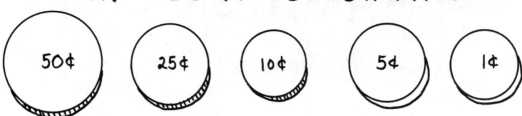

Arrange and count coins in the space above. Record work below.

1. Find one way to
   make change for **29¢**

   Another way

2. Find one way to
   make change for **55¢**

   Another way

3. Find one way to
   make change for **78¢**

   Another way

4. Find one way to
   make change for **91¢**

   Another way

5. Make your own
   problem here.

From Exploring Mathematics: Activities for Concept and Skill Development, Copyright © 1990 Scott, Foresman and Company.

Teaching Aid 3.5a

MAKING CHANGE

Figure out ways to make change for each total. Use exactly the number of coins called for in each problem. Figure out how to do each problem at least 2 different ways.

1. Make change for 50¢ using 5 coins.

2. Make change for 75¢ using 5 coins.

3. Make change for 75¢ using 8 coins.

4. Make change for $1.00 using 11 coins.

5. Make a money problem for your classmates. Make sure your problem can be solved at least 2 different ways.

FUNNY MONEY

Teaching Aid 3.6   Have children color the "money" in gray, brown, and green tones.

From Exploring Mathematics: Activities for Concept and Skill Development, Copyright © 1990 Scott, Foresman and Company.

4

Think, Then Push Buttons: Calculators for Young Children

Calculators, modern technological aids to computation, can help young children develop both mathematical concepts and skills. Researchers have found that the calculator is a powerful teaching and learning tool. Calculator usage often takes the emphasis off computation and lets children concentrate on understanding numerical relationships and focus on the problem-solving process.

On the other hand, calculator usage *does* require thinking as children select appropriate numbers and operations to enter into the calculator and as they judge and interpret the calculator's answers.

Most children are familiar with calculators, having seen older children and adults using them. Nevertheless, you might ask—before doing calculator activities—whether the children have used a calculator before. You might also help the children compare two or three calculator models, noting their many similarities and few differences. Teach the children how to care for their calculators as you show them how to work the electronic marvels.

If you have a situation in which each child or pair of children has a calculator, the class can work on the following activities in a large group. The activities are also suitable for small-group work or even individual work in a learning center. Although they are intended for use with calculators, most of the activities in this chapter may also be done "by hand."

GETTING ACQUAINTED WITH CALCULATORS

Although most children have grown up seeing calculators in use, they still need some orientation before they are ready to use calculators independently.

Objective: Children will become acquainted with calculators through discussion, demonstration, and research.

Materials: Posterboard or paper to make a large calculator model from Teaching Aid 4.1, scissors, markers, calculators, newspaper or catalog ads for calculators.

Preparing for the Activities: Choose pertinent activities from the ones listed below. Secure materials as needed. Make a large calculator model.

Approximate Time Frame: 10 to 30 minutes per activity.

Conducting the Activities: Conduct several of the following introductory activities over a period of several days.

Show the children at least two calculator models, and have them compare keys and general appearance.

Invite an upper elementary student to talk to the children about using calculators. Have the older child demonstrate use of a calculator in some simple problems.

Have an adult visitor talk to the children about using the calculator in his or her job or home.

As a homework assignment, have the children interview at least five people to find out whether they use calculators, and, if so, how they use them. Lead a discussion about what the children found; you might even make a graph of the results.

Provide ads from newspapers, catalogs, and magazines, and have the children search for pictures of calculators. They could then cut out the pictures and create several collages based on calculator prices— e.g., calculators priced under $10, calculators priced $10 to $50, and calculators priced over $50.

Open a calculator and let the children examine the backs of the keys and the many tiny circuits.

Use Teaching Aid 4.1 (or an enlargement of it) when talking to the children about parts of the calculator. Help them identify the keyboard, function keys, number keys, on-off switch (if any), display,

From *Exploring Mathematics: Activities for Concept and Skill Development,* Copyright © 1990 Scott, Foresman and Company.

and battery compartment (if any). Call out a variety of simple math problems, and have the children show on the model the various keys they would press to solve the problems.

Discuss careful handling of the calculator. Explain to the children that calculators should be kept clean and never handled with greasy or sticky hands. Tell them that calculators should be used on a flat surface to prevent dropping and should always be turned off when not in use.

Evaluating the Activities: Assess the children's attention, interest, and participation.

Extending the Activities: Let the children look at and/or read books about the history of calculating devices. Provide opportunities for interested children to observe an adult who uses calculators in a workplace.

MAKE ME COUNT

Children may gain insight into the process of counting as they learn a new calculator skill in this activity.

Objective: Children will make the calculator "count" forward and backward by adding and subtracting values and by repeating use of the equals key.

Materials: Hundreds chart, transparency paper to reproduce worksheet (Teaching Aid 4.2), calculators.

Preparing for the Activity: Duplicate the hundreds chart transparency. Duplicate a worksheet for each child.

Approximate Time Frame: 15 to 20 minutes.

Conducting the Activity: Project the hundreds chart on the chalkboard. Ask the children to count by ones for several numbers from 25 (25, 26, 27, 28, 29, 30, 31, etc.). Have a volunteer child circle the numbers as the class says them. Then have the class practice counting from other starting points by other numbers. For example, start at 37 and count by threes for six numbers (37, 40, 43, 46, 49, 52, 55).

Look at the patterns that are created in the chart. Ask the children how they know what the answers will be. Some may suggest that you skip every other number on the chart when counting by twos; others may say that you add on twos.

Practice several examples of counting backwards by ones, twos, and other numbers. Discuss different ways of thinking about the process of counting backwards—"skipping" backwards or subtracting.

Now let the children use a calculator to count. For example, to count by twos starting at 22, a child would press 22, plus, 2, equals, and get the answer: 24. Then pressing plus, 2, and equals, the child will produce the next number: 26. Let the children practice other examples. Next, ask the children to predict what their answers will be if they start at 38 and count by fives for five numbers (38, 43, 48, 53, 58, 63). Record some of their predictions, and then let the children try it.

At this point, introduce the idea that most calculators will count when even fewer keys are pressed. To count by ones from 1, press 1, plus, 1, equals, equals, equals, equals, equals, and see the calculator count to 6. Let the children see if they can figure out how to make the calculator count by twos from 1 (press 1, plus, 2, equals, equals, equals, equals, equals, etc.).

Have the children complete the worksheet (Teaching Aid 4.2). Check their answers and let them share some of their problems and answers for number 7.

Evaluating the Activity: Listen to the children's discussion in order to gain insight into their thinking about patterns. Check the worksheets.

Extending the Activity: Encourage the children to do similar counting problems by hand or on the calculator. Start counting at zero to practice multiples of a given number. For example, if you count by fives from zero, you will use the multiples of 5: 0, 5, 10, 15, 20, etc. Count backwards from multiples of a number too. For example, counting backwards from 48 by sixes (48, 42, 36, 30, 24, . . .) lets children practice multiples of 6.

FIGURE YOUR CHANGE

This activity combines calculating, thinking, and counting money in realistic situations.

Objectives: Children will locate prices on a menu, figure totals of "orders" on a calculator, calculate change, and count out money for the change.

Materials: Paper to duplicate menus (Teaching Aid 4.3a and b) and task cards (Teaching Aid 4.3c), play money or real coins or "Funny Money" duplicated from Teaching Aid 3.6, calculator for each group of four to five children, scissors.

From *Exploring Mathematics: Activities for Concept and Skill Development*, Copyright © 1990 Scott, Foresman and Company.

Preparing for the Activity: Duplicate the menus and task cards. If no tax is charged in restaurants in your state, blank out the note about tax on the menu.

Approximate Time Frame: 30 to 40 minutes.

Conducting the Activity: Organize the children into groups of four or five. Give each group two menus, a set of task cards, and a set of "money." Show the children how to take turns selecting task cards, "ordering," and figuring their total. Discuss with the children that because most orders have a limit for the total, they will have to estimate their total before they order.

Instruct the children to figure their change on the calculator and then to role-play paying for their order and receiving change. Circulate around the room to spot-check the children and listen to their reasoning.

Evaluating the Activity: Assign a problem similar to the ones that the children have practiced and assess each child's solution to the problem. Spot-check the children to see who handles the calculator with ease and who counts change ably. For additional practice, let the children work with advertisements to "buy" products and count their change.

Extending the Activity: Let the children work from real local menus to order, figure totals, and receive change. This activity could be set up in a learning center for independent practice. Invite the children to design menus and task cards and then to conduct the activity based on their creative ideas.

$$+ \div \times - + - \times \div +$$

WORKING WITH PLACE VALUE

This activity emphasizes the idea that place value makes a big difference in numbers. A seven in the ones place is very different from a seven in the hundreds place!

Objective: Children will apply their knowledge of place value to change the values of numbers on the calculator.

Materials: Calculators (one for each child or pair of children).

Preparing for the Activity: Secure a calculator for each child or pair of children. Perhaps the children could bring calculators from home if none are available on a regular basis at school.

Approximate Time Frame: 15 to 20 minutes.

Conducting the Activity: Dictate several numbers for the children to enter into the calculator. Pronounce the numbers carefully once, and then pronounce them again for the children to check what they have entered. Have a child write each number on the board for an extra check.
Then present problems such as the following:

Enter 358. Change the number to read 350 by a subtraction. [Subtract 8]

Enter 718. Make the calculator read 728 by an addition. [Add 10]

Enter 543. Change the display to read 500 by one or two subtractions. [Subtract 40 and then 3, or subtract 43]

Enter 257. Change the value to 100. [Subtract 157, or subtract 100 and then 50 and then 7]

Encourage the children to discuss the strategies they used in solving the problems.

Evaluating the Activity: Observe the children and determine who follows directions successfully and who expresses ideas about how to work the problems.

Extending the Activity: Let the children suggest problems for their classmates to work. Extend the problems to include larger numbers.

PUT IN THE SIGNS

Objectives: Children will analyze problems, put in operation signs to produce answers, and check their work on a calculator.

Materials: Paper to reproduce worksheets, a calculator for each pair of children or one or two calculators to use in a learning center.

Preparing for the Activities Duplicate Teaching Aid 4.4a (for advanced first graders or second graders) or Teaching Aid 4.4b (for second or third graders).

Approximate Time Frame: 30 minutes.

Conducting the Activity: Show the children the following problem:

$$2\ 8\ 4 = 14$$

Ask them to try various operation signs to make the problem work correctly: 2 + 8 + 4 = 14.

From *Exploring Mathematics: Activities for Concept and Skill Development*, Copyright © 1990 Scott, Foresman and Company.

Then ask them what they might do with this problem:

$$2\ 8\ 4 = 24$$

See if they can figure out that the solution is $28 - 4 = 24$.

Have the children complete the worksheet you have selected. Emphasize the importance of thinking through the problems first, and then using the calculator to check results.

Students doing the problems on Teaching Aid 4.4a should get the following answers:

1. $6 + 0 + 5 = 11$
2. $4 + 2 + 10 = 16$
3. $12 + 3 = 15$
4. $1 + 0 + 6 = 7$
5. $13 - 2 = 11$
6. $15 - 7 = 8$
7. $20 - 11 = 9$
8. $14 - 12 = 2$
9. $2 + 3 + 5 - 2 = 8$
10. $(10 + 2) - 11 = 1$
11. $18 + 2 + (5 - 5) = 20$
12. $(4 - 0) + 26 = 30$

Students doing the problems on Teaching Aid 4.4b should get the following answers:

1. $8 + 8 + 8 = 24$
2. $88 + 8 = 96$
3. $39 + 2 + 24 = 65$
4. $50 + 23 = 73$
5. $105 - 19 = 86$
6. $280 - 14 = 266$
7. $300 - 124 = 176$
8. $96 - 24 = 72$
9. $(2 \times 6) \div 3 = 4$
10. $(2 + 6) - 3 = 5$
11. $(19 + 3) \times 2 = 44$
12. $(15 - 2) - 10 = 3$

Evaluating the Activity: Check the children's worksheets. Watch the children as they work and determine who operates the calculator with ease and who needs additional practice and guidance.

Extending the Activity: Invite the children to make similar problems for each other. You might post some of their suggestions in a "Puzzle Corner" or "Calculator Corner."

÷ ✕ − + − ✕ ÷

CHAPTER 4

TEACHING AIDS

÷ ✕ − + − ✕ ÷

CALCULATOR PICTURE

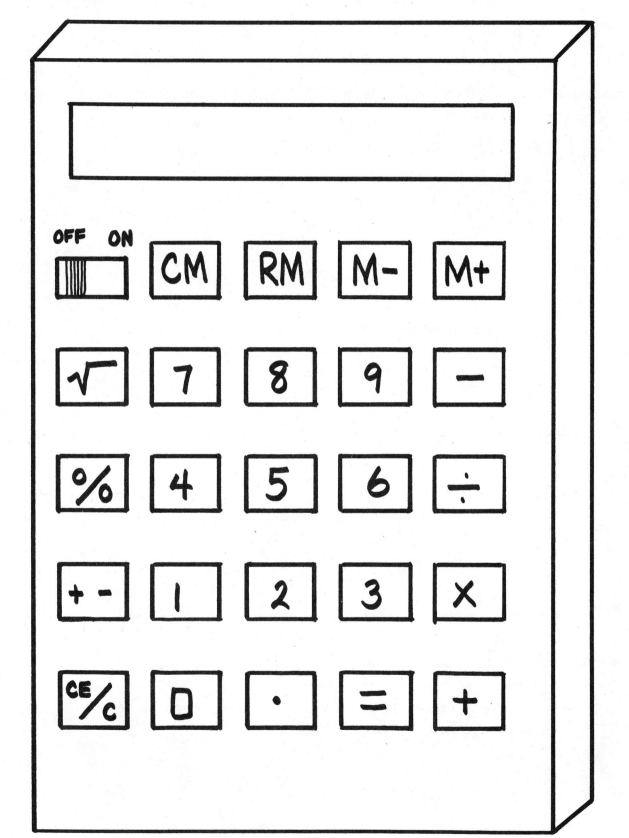

Teaching Aid 4.1

MAKE ME COUNT!

2...4...6...8...

Study each problem. Decide what the last number will be. Write your prediction in the blank. Now make your calculator count. Record the numbers you get in the blanks. Check the last number with your prediction.

Make me count by 2's.

1. _____ , _____ , _____ , _____ , _____
                                              prediction _____

2. _____ , _____ , _____ , _____ , _____
                                              prediction _____

Make me count backwards by 5's.

3. _____ , _____ , _____ , _____
                                              prediction _____

4. _____ , _____ , _____ , _____
                                              prediction _____

Can you make me double the number?

5. _____ , _____ , _____ , _____
                                              prediction _____

6. _____ , _____ , _____ , _____
                                              prediction _____

Make your own problem. Let a classmate solve it.

7.

Beverages

Milk	40¢
Cola	50¢
Root Beer	50¢
Milk Shakes	75¢
chocolate or vanilla	
Orange Juice	50¢

Tax is included in our prices.

GRANT'S

GIANT

Burgers

Things To Drink

Milk	
Chocolate	50¢
White	50¢
Cola	60¢
Bubbly Soda	60¢
Fruit Punch	50¢
Root Beer	60¢
Water	free

Tax is included
in our special prices.

Teaching Aid 4.3a

PIZZAS
by
PAUL

**Deluxe Pizzas
with our
Personal Touch...**

Our GIANT Burgers

Single		$1.00
Double		$1.25
Triple		$1.50

Burger Toppings

Catsup, mustard, pickles, onions	free
Cheese	10¢
Chili	25¢
Tomatoes	5¢
Sour Cream	10¢

Extras

Crispy French Fries	50¢
Salad	
small	50¢
large	$1.00
Fruit Pies	50¢
Cookies	30¢
Fresh Fruit	
apple	25¢
orange	25¢
banana	20¢

Personalize your pizza choosing from these sizes and toppings:

15 cm (6 in.)	30 cm (12 in.)
$3.00	$5.00

Toppings

Extra Cheese	50¢
Olives	25¢
Hamburger	50¢
Sausage	50¢
Tuna	25¢
Special house topping	$1.00

Teaching Aid 4.3b

Instead of a Pizza...

Spaghetti

with tomatoes and cheese	$1.50
with meat sauce	$2.00
vegetable deluxe	$2.50

With Your Pizza...

Salad	
small	50¢
large	$1.00
Special Garlic Bread -- 2 large slices	50¢

From Exploring Mathematics: Activities for Concept and Skill Development, Copyright © 1990 Scott, Foresman and Company.

FIGURE YOUR CHANGE

Task Cards

Funny Money
①

Order a small sausage pizza with extra cheese.

Also order 2 drinks.

Calculate your total bill. Count your change from $10.00.

Order a sandwich with one topping, french fries, and a drink. Order one more thing if you can keep your order under $3.00.

Find your total.

Figure and count out your change.

Order a small pizza with the special house topping, a large hamburger pizza, and 4 drinks. Order 2 salads also.

What is your change from $20.00?

Make an order for two -- sandwiches, salad, and beverages. Use the calculator to figure your total. Find your change from $10.00. Count out your change.

Make an order for 4 hungry people, but keep it under $25.00

Figure your total. Count out your change.

You have $20.00 to order for 5 people. Order whatever you want!

Find your total. Count out your change from $20.00.

Write your own problem.

Teaching Aid 4.3c

Teaching
Aid 4.4a

Use + and = signs here.

1. 6 0 5 = 11   2. 4 2 1 0 = 16

3. 1 2 3 1 5   4. 1 0 6 7

Use - and = signs here.

5. 1 3 2 = 11   6. 1 5 7 = 8

7. 2 0 1 1 9   8. 1 4 1 2 2

Use +, -, and = signs here.

9. 2 3 5 2 = 8   10. 1 0 2 1 1 = 1

11. 1 8 2 5 5 20   12. 4 0 2 6 30

From *Exploring Mathematics: Activities for Concept and Skill Development*, Copyright © 1990 Scott, Foresman and Company.

Use + and = signs here.

1. 8 8 8 = 24   2. 8 8 8 = 96

3. 3 9 22 4 65   4. 5 0 2 3 7 3

Use − and = signs here.

5. 1 0 5 1 9 = 86   6. 2 8 0 14 = 266

7. 300 1 24 176   8. 9 6 24 72

Use +, −, ×, ÷, and = signs here.

9. 2 6 3 4   10. 2 6 3 5

11. 1 9 3 2 44   12. 1 5 2 1 0 3

Teaching Aid 4.4b

5
Parts and Wholes: Beginning Fractions

"Some of us are wearing blue." "Part of the pennies shows heads; the other part shows tails." "I can zip my coat in just a fraction of a minute." "Your part is bigger than mine!" "I have half a cookie." "I'm gonna eat the *whole* thing!"

Statements like these, used in everyday life, demonstrate children's intuitive knowledge of fractions. Educators can build on this informal knowledge of relationships of parts and wholes as they encourage and deepen children's understanding of the meanings of fractions.

As children extend their knowledge of fractions, they need to use many models. Fraction symbols and fraction names can then be associated with the models in meaningful ways. Children can compare parts to wholes and parts to other parts, thus working with equivalence and order of fractions. They can even work informally with addition and subtraction of fractional numbers. Through concrete activities done over a period of time, fractions and their symbols become meaningful to children.

Although working with parts of wholes is the meaning of fractions that young children find easiest to understand, they can be successfully exposed to other meanings: quotients and ratios. Fractions are quotients or division problems—e.g., a child with two cookies who divides them among four people finds that each person gets 2/4 or 1/2 cookie. Ratios present comparisons—e.g., since each child in the classroom has two shoes, the ratio of children to shoes is 1 to 2; similarly, the ratio of fingers to children is 10 to 1.

The varied activities in this chapter present fractions in the context of the children themselves, manipulatives, recipes, and pictures. The concrete aids will help ensure success with subsequent, more formal work with fractions.

FRACTIONS OF THE CLASS

Fractions take on real meaning when they are used to describe relationships among class members.

Objective: Children will gain experience naming and writing fractions that apply to relationships within their class.

Materials: Paper to duplicate worksheets from Teaching Aid 5.1.

Preparing for the Activity: Duplicate copies of the worksheet.

Approximate Time Frame: 30 minutes.

Conducting the Activity: Introduce "all," "part," and "none" as ways to describe relationships among the children in your class. Have the children tell you which relational word applies in the following situations:

> Who is taller than two feet? [probably all]
> Who is shorter than six feet? [probably all]
> Who is wearing glasses? [probably part]
> Who is male? [probably part]
> Who is wearing purple sequined shoes? [probably none]
> Who has brought a dog to the classroom today? [probably none]

Describe to the children how we use fractions to be specific about parts. Call five children up to the front. Ask them for examples that involve specific fractions about themselves—e.g., two out of the five are wearing jeans or 1/5 of them has tie shoes. Show the children how to write the fractions, and let them take turns writing appropriate fractions on the chalkboard. Vary the number of children at the front of the class in order to demonstrate different denominators.

Write specific fractions based on characteristics of the entire class. Then have the children complete the worksheet, and check their answers. Let them discuss some of their answers for the last two problems.

Evaluating the Activity: Notice whether the children seem to understand the all/part/none relationships. Check the children's worksheets to see if they have counted and written fractions correctly.

Extending the Activity: Encourage the children to use fractions to describe other relationships among class members. Later, when you make and interpret graphs, use fractions to describe relationships of categories.

From *Exploring Mathematics: Activities for Concept and Skill Development,* Copyright © 1990 Scott, Foresman and Company.

CAKES AND HAMBURGERS

Children can use these "yummy" manipulatives and worksheets to gain a concrete understanding of fractions and their relationships.

Objectives: Children will use two different fractional models to show fractional parts and verify equivalent fractional relationships.

Materials: Paper to duplicate worksheets from Teaching Aid 5.2, transparency to reproduce the cake worksheet (optional), pellon or felt to make felt board pieces similar to cakes and hamburgers (optional), crayons, scissors.

Preparing for the Activities: Duplicate the worksheets from Teaching Aid 5.2a, b, c. You might also make felt board pieces that look like cakes and hamburgers or a transparency of the cake worksheet for demonstration with the children.

Approximate Time Frame: 20 minutes per worksheet.

Conducting the Activities: Show and explain to the children each of the following tasks. Let them complete and discuss the worksheets.

Cakes. Show the children how a cake could be cut into two equal pieces. Show the drawings below, and have the children name the ones that show halves. Encourage the children to suggest other ways that a cake could be cut into halves.

Let the children complete the first cake worksheet. Discuss the fourths and eighths that are shown in the second problem. Then introduce the second cake worksheet which shows a cake cut in fifths. Let the children cut out the candles and then complete the worksheet.

Hamburgers. Introduce the worksheet and let the children complete it. Discuss the children's work. Next, let the children cut out their hamburgers and work in small groups on questions such as the following:

If each child puts any two hamburgers into a pile in a central area, what fraction of the hamburgers have seeds on the buns? (Encourage answers such as "all," "most," "some," or "none." Let each group also give a specific answer to the question. If five children work together, perhaps the answer is 3/10 of the hamburgers.)

If each child puts a "favorite" kind of hamburger into the pile, how many hamburgers have mustard on them? What fraction is this? If each child puts three hamburgers into the pile, what fraction of the hamburgers have lettuce on them?

Here are the answers to Teaching Aid 5.2a, b, and c:

5.2a
1. The first and second cakes show halves.
2. Answers will vary.
3. Answers will vary.

5.2b
1. Color one section yellow.
2. Color any two sections brown.
3. 2/5
4. 4/5
5. 3/5
6. 5/5 or all

5.2c
1. Three hamburgers should be colored with lettuce.
2. Four hamburger buns should be colored with seeds.
3. One hamburger should be colored with catsup.
4. Two hamburgers should have soft drinks drawn beside them.
5. Answers will vary.

Evaluating the Activities: Watch the children as they work and listen to their comments. Assess their understanding of fraction concepts.

Extending the Activities: Encourage the children to make additional problems to go with the worksheets. Discuss other foods that are commonly divided into pieces. Ask several "fractions of the class" problems: What fraction of the class actually likes lettuce on hamburgers? What fraction of the class likes chocolate best as a frosting flavor?

FRACTION SEARCH

Fractions are all around us! These activities provide a variety of ways for children to explore fractions.

From *Exploring Mathematics: Activities for Concept and Skill Development*, Copyright © 1990 Scott, Foresman and Company.

Objectives: Children will draw and identify pictures that represent fractions. Children will search for uses of fractions at home and interview people to see how adults use fractions.

Materials: Paper, crayons, pencils.

Preparing for the Activities: Decide which activities to use with the children.

Approximate Time Frame: 20 minutes per activity.

Conducting the Activities: Show the children how to do any of the following activities. Let them show and discuss their completed work.

Fraction Drawings. Have the children draw pictures of various objects and containers that are about half full. Challenge the children to draw things that no else would think of.

Ask the children to draw something that could be divided into eight parts. They should color a small fraction of the parts—except for 0/8, a small fraction for which *no* parts could be colored.

Next, have the children draw something that could be divided into many pieces and then color in a large fraction of the pieces. Help the children name the fractional parts they have drawn.

Pick A Fraction. Show the children how to examine ads and pick out fractional relationships. For instance, an ad may show four watches, three with second hands. Have the children say or write sentences about the relationship they see: "3/4 of the watches have second hands." Post the labeled ads on a bulletin board.

Kitchen Cabinet Fraction Search. Ask the children to look in their kitchen cabinets and find and record at least five examples of the use of fractions. For example, the children might report "We have six cups and seven saucers. 6/13 of the items are cups; 7/13 are saucers. The ratio of cups to saucers is 6 to 7." Or, "I found a can of peaches that has four 1/2-cup servings in it."

Interviewing. Have the children interview three or four adults, asking about all the ways the adults use fractions. Compute the results in a long list on the chalkboard. Or, let the children select some interview questions and report their results in fractions. For example, a child might report that five out of the 12 people interviewed had suffered a broken bone or that six out of the seven adults interviewed drank coffee regularly.

Evaluating the Activities: Spot-check the children's results. Note their conversations to see if they use fraction names correctly.

Extending the Activities: Let the children suggest other formats for fraction searches. Use their suggestions for group or class activities.

COOKING WITH FRACTIONS

Objective: Small groups of children will work cooperatively to prepare recipes that use fractional measurements.

Materials: Paper to duplicate recipes from Teaching Aids 5.3a and b. For the fudge recipe: confectioners sugar, peanut butter, cocoa, milk, vanilla, bowl, pie or cake pan. For the painted toast recipe: white bread, milk, small bowls or cups, food color, clean paint brushes, toaster oven. Each recipe requires measuring cups and paper to reproduce the recipe; the fudge recipe requires a 2.5ml (1/2-teaspoon) measuring spoon.

Preparing for the Activities: Choose one of the recipes and gather the necessary supplies and equipment. Children or parents might be willing to contribute various ingredients, but be sure to allow several days for the supplies to be brought in. Duplicate, color, and laminate a recipe chart from Teaching Aid 5.3a or b.

Approximate Time Frame: 30 minutes per recipe.

Conducting the Activities: Work with a small group of children to prepare each recipe. Show the children the divisions on the measuring cups and the markings on the spoons. Help them read the recipe chart, examine the pictures, and try to use the measuring tools independently. Encourage careful measuring to make the recipe "turn out" right. "No-Cook Metric Fudge" makes 20 to 30 pieces—enough for each child in a small group to sample and take home a few pieces. "Painted Toast" makes a nourishing, inexpensive, and quick snack!

On subsequent days (or later the same day), let other small groups prepare the same recipe until every child has had a chance.

Evaluating the Activities: Observe the children's cooperation and level of independence in making measurements.

Extending the Activities: Make other recipes that use fractional measurements. Ask the children to help prepare a recipe at home and report on the results.

÷ ✕ − + − ✕ ÷

CHAPTER

TEACHING

AIDS

FRACTIONS of the Class

Count the numbers of classmates for each situation. Fill in the blanks.

About children in your row or work group:

Fraction

1. _____ out of _____ have a pet at home. _____

2. _____ out of _____ are wearing jewelry today. _____

3. _____ out of _____ are writing with pens. _____

4. _____ out of _____ are wearing boots. _____

About children in the entire class:

5. _____ out of _____ classmates have blue eyes. _____

6. _____ out of _____ classmates are wearing belts. _____

7. _____ out of _____ classmates have at least 1 spiral notebook. _____

8. _____ out of _____ classmates are wearing red today. _____

Fill in your own sentences and fractions.

9. _____ _____

10. _____ _____

Teaching Aid 5.1

From Exploring Mathematics: Activities for Concept and Skill Development, Copyright © 1990 Scott, Foresman and Company.

Fractions of a CAKE

1. Color the cakes that show halves. Do not color the cakes that don't show halves. Label each half with the fraction ½.

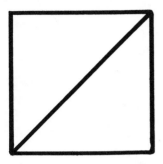
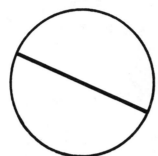
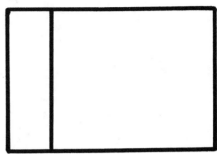

2. Color half of each cake brown and half red.

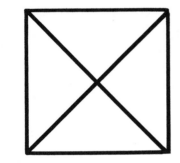
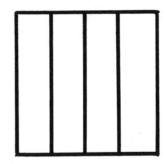
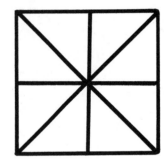

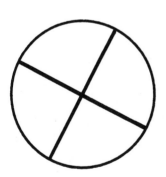

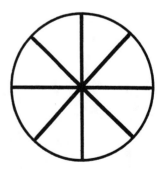

3. Draw a line segment to divide each cake in half. Color the halves two different colors.

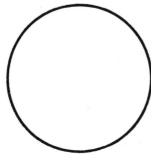

Teaching Aid 5.2 a

Fractions of a CAKE

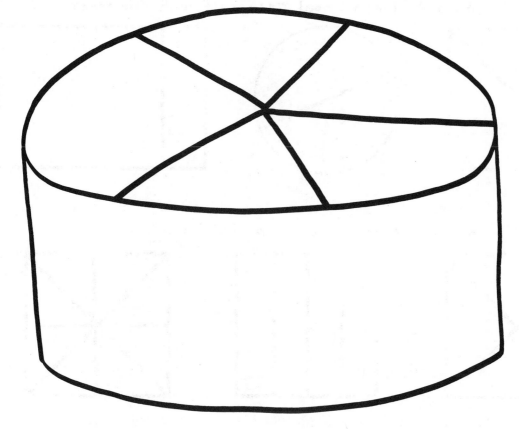

Teaching Aid 5.2b

From *Exploring Mathematics: Activities for Concept and Skill Development*, Copyright © 1990 Scott, Foresman and Company.

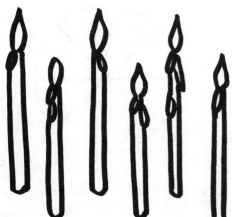

1. Color $\frac{1}{5}$ of the cake yellow like lemon frosting.

2. Color $\frac{2}{5}$ of the cake brown like chocolate frosting.

3. What fraction of the cake is left? _____ Color it any color you wish.

4. Place candles on $\frac{1}{5}$ of the cake pieces. What fraction of the pieces <u>doesn't</u> have candles? _____

5. Place candles on $\frac{2}{5}$. What fraction doesn't have candles? _____

6. Glue candles on all the pieces. What fraction has candles? _____

• FRACTIONS with HAMBURGERS •

Teaching Aid 5.2c

1. Color lettuce on $\frac{3}{8}$ of the hamburgers.

2. Draw seeds on $\frac{1}{2}$ of the buns.   3. Draw catsup on $\frac{5}{8}$ of the burgers.

4. Draw soft drinks beside $\frac{1}{4}$ of the burgers.

5. Color mustard on any part of the hamburgers. Write the fraction. ____

Mix in a bowl:

 2 c. (500 mℓ) confectioners
    sugar

 $\frac{1}{2}$ c. (125 mℓ) peanut butter

 $\frac{1}{4}$ c. (60 mℓ) cocoa

 $\frac{1}{4}$ c. (60 mℓ) milk

 $\frac{1}{2}$ t. (2.5 mℓ) vanilla

Press into a pan. When firm, cut into 20-30 pieces.

From Exploring Mathematics: Activities for Concept and Skill Development, Copyright © 1990 Scott, Foresman and Company.

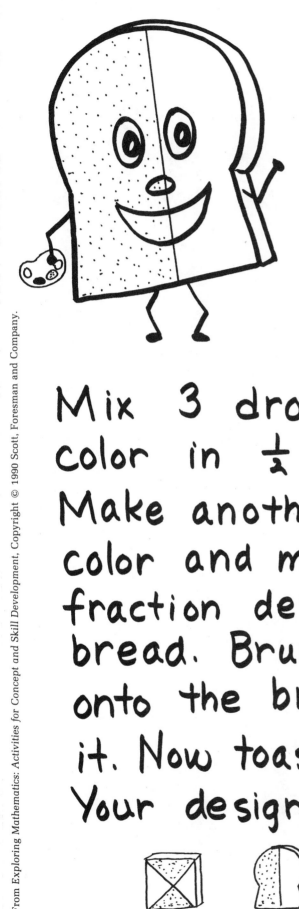

PAINTED TOAST !

Mix 3 drops of food color in $\frac{1}{2}$ cup of milk. Make another color of food color and milk. Plan a fraction design for your bread. Brush milk lightly onto the bread. Don't soak it. Now toast your bread. Your design will show!

Teaching Aid 5.3 b

6

Picturing, Comparing, and Summarizing Data: Graphing

Children are surrounded by data! Graphing helps children categorize and organize data, thus making sense of all the numbers. Graphs give children a visual picture of data. Children find it easy to look at a graph and see larger and smaller sets. On some graphs, children may notice empty sets too.

Children are always interested in their own opinions and those of their classmates. The graphing experiences that follow—which can be personalized and individualized to show data about your own class—encourage children to express their opinions and let them know you value their opinions. Since making and interpreting graphs also foster decision-making, graphing experiences are generally quite valuable for young children.

But doesn't graphing involve a lot of time and effort to prepare all kinds of grids and markers? Not necessarily! Many of the graphs described in the following activities involve reusable markers and reusable (or easily duplicated) grids. They're simple either to use as they are or to alter to fit the needs of your students.

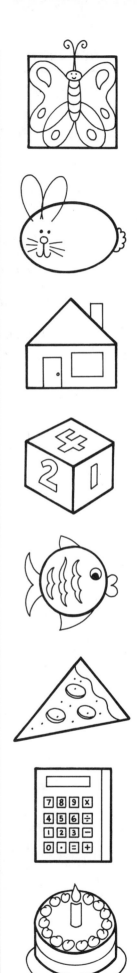

FILL-IN-THE-BLANK GRAPHS

These graphs can be done in the bar graph format, either horizontally or vertically. Children should have experience with both types of bar graphs.

Objective: Children will make and interpret a bar graph.

Materials: Paper, scissors, ruler, crayons or markers.

Preparing for the Activity: Cut a 10x10cm (4x4-inch) square of paper for each child. Decide on a graph topic.

Approximate Time Frame: 20 minutes.

Conducting the Activity: Present the graph topic and categories to the children. Have each child draw a picture and glue it onto a large sheet of paper. Lead the children in interpreting the graph by comparing categories and counting the total number of graph markers. Help the children make fractional statements about the graph—e.g., "About half of the markers are in one category"; or "Out of the 27 children in the class, five chose a particular category."

Here are some topics for fill-in-the-blank graphs:

Number of Legs. Ask the children to draw pictures of real or fanciful animals. Tell them that the animals must have two, four, six, eight, or more than eight legs. Graph the results, showing how many animals were drawn in each category.

After-School Activities. Let the children make up categories based on what they do after school—e.g., watch TV, play, shop, do school work. Graph the results, showing how many children do each after-school activity.

Food Groups. Have the children draw or cut out small pictures of their favorite foods and then categorize the foods by the four basic groups: meats, fruits and vegetables, breads and cereals, and milk products. Graph the results.

Evaluating the Activity: Make certain that the children correctly categorize their pictures. Assess the children's participation in the discussion and their use of fractional comparisons.

Extending the Activity: Make additional fill-in-the-blank graphs using current events or topics you are studying in science, reading, or social studies.

From Exploring Mathematics: Activities for Concept and Skill Development, Copyright © 1990 Scott, Foresman and Company.

PUPIL POLLS

Two or three pupils can become pollsters and show their classmates' opinions on a graph. Young pollsters develop pride and responsibility as they do their work.

Objectives: A small group of children will help to develop a graph topic and graph categories. They will poll their classmates and present their results to the class.

Materials: Paper to duplicate Teaching Aid 6.1, a clip board or piece of cardboard and clothespins to make a clip board.

Preparing for the Activity: Duplicate a graph grid. Furnish a clip board or clip the grid to a piece of cardboard with clothespins.

Approximate Time Frame: 20 minutes.

Conducting the Activity: Meet briefly with two or three children to decide on a topic for the poll and to develop categories for it. Help the children write the category names on the grid, perhaps color-coding them or drawing a little picture of each category.

   Let the student pollsters move quietly around the classroom, asking each classmate for an opinion. Help the pollsters plan a brief "show and tell" session in which they share their poll results with the class. Repeat with other students and different topics until all have had a turn.

Evaluating the Activity: Check the graph with the children. Have them compare categories and tell the main ideas that the graph shows. See if the children give a clear report to their classmates.

Extending the Activity: Help the children develop topics so that they can poll people at their homes. Encourage a group of student pollsters to go to another classroom and take a poll.

REUSABLE GRAPHS

Reusable graphs and graph forms make the teacher's work easy because they can be used again and again with simple modifications.

Objectives: Children will make and interpret bar and picture graphs.

Materials: For the clothespin graph: paper, a clothespin for each child, marker, scissors. For the felt face graph: felt in appropriate skin tones to make a face for each child, yarn and glue (optional), scissors, marker, felt board. For the milk carton graph: a clean milk carton for each child, transparent tape, construction paper, scissors, clear contact paper (optional), a photo of each child (could be done by taking a group picture and then cutting individual photos apart). For the stand-on graph: two to four rolls of plastic shelf paper, ruler or meter stick, permanent marker, paper to make category markers.

Preparing for the Activities: Decide on graph topics. Duplicate and gather the materials needed for the type of graph you select.

Approximate Time Frame: 15 to 20 minutes.

Conducting the Activities: Let the children take turns placing their markers in the category of their choosing. Help the children interpret the graph by asking an open-ended question—e.g., "What does this graph tell us?" Invite several children to express their answers.

Follow up with specific questions not covered by the children—e.g., "Which category has more markers?" "Do any categories have the same number of markers?" "How can you tell?" "The graph represents data from how many children?" "One category (specify which one) has how many more people than another?"

Choose from the following types of reusable graphs:

Clothespin Graph. Have each child write his or her name on a clothespin. Make a rectangular graph form 15x30cm (6x12 inches) marked with a title and two category names. Pass the form around and let each child place a clothespin on the appropriate side, starting at the bottom. Teaching Aid 6.2a shows two examples—"Do You Have a Pet" and "Are You Wearing a Belt"—with sides labeled yes and no. Here are some other suggestions: "I'm a . . ." (label the sides boy and girl), "Will It Rain Before Friday?" (label the sides yes and no; then use this graph early in the week so that the class can compare its predictions with the weather later in the week), "I'd Rather Eat . . ." (label the sides hot dogs and hamburgers, apples and oranges, plain peanut butter sandwiches and peanut butter/jelly sandwiches, etc.).

Felt Face Graphs. Using the pattern on Teaching Aid 6.2b, cut a face for each child out of felt in appropriate colors for the skin tones of your students. If you wish, you can have the children glue yarn on the tops of the faces for hair. Make a category marker and title for the graph, and then have the children place their felt face markers in the appropriate category. Line up the markers as you count them, and use the markers to create both vertical and horizontal bar graphs.

Here are some topics for felt face graphs: "Number of People in My Family" (use categories from two to six or more), "How I Travel to School" (possible categories include walk, bike, ride bus, ride in car), "My Favorite Book This Week" (use titles of books read during the week as categories), "Color of My Socks" (categories indicated by sock shapes in various colors).

Milk Carton Picture Graphs. Help children flatten the tops of clean milk cartons to make the cartons into block shapes. Instruct them to cover the tops of the milk cartons with a strip of paper, wrap the carton with another strip, and then tape the paper in place. Finally, tape a photograph of each child to one side of his or her carton. You might then cover the picture with clear contact paper. Teaching Aid 6.2b illustrates the procedure.

Have the children use their picture markers for graph topics such as these: "Where I Live" (choices could include house, apartment, condo or trailer), "My Favorite Pet" (categories might be dog, cat, horse, fish), "I'd Rather Drink . . . " (use milk, chocolate milk, and juices as choices), "I Help at Home By . . ." (ask the children for categories).

Stand-On Graph. The children themselves act as graph markers for this simple type of graph! Unroll a 4-meter (12-foot) roll of plastic shelf paper and mark it into sections about 40cm (15 inches) wide with a permanent marker. Use one section for each graph category. Then invite half the students to stand (or sit) on the appropriate category section; the other students watch and interpret the graph results. A stand-on graph is illustrated in Teaching Aid 6.2b.

Possible topics for the stand-on graph include: "My Shirt or Top Pattern" (choices might be solid, striped, plaid), "My Hair Color" (use colors appropriate to your students), "Length of My Name" (mark off categories for fewer than five letters, five letters, and more than five letters).

Evaluating the Activities: Observe whether the children work cooperatively and seem to make independent decisions. Assess their voluntary responses about the graphs, and note their responses to direct questions.

Extending the Activities: Use the children's suggestions for additional graph topics.

EASY FINGERPRINT GRAPH

This graph is really personalized! Although each person's fingerprints are unique, they can be grouped by type. In this easy activity, children make non-smear fingerprints without an ink pad.

Objectives: Children will make, observe, and classify thumb prints and graph the results. Children will also label each print by type.

Materials: Paper to reproduce worksheets (Teaching Aid 6.3) and graph grid from Teaching Aid 6.1, pencils, two to four rolls of transparent tape.

Preparing for the Activity: Duplicate a copy of the worksheet for each child. Duplicate a graph grid.

Approximate Time Frame: 30 to 40 minutes.

Conducting the Activity: Take the children through the four steps for making non-smear fingerprints:

1. Scribble over a scrap of paper with a pencil.
2. Rub a fingertip over the pencil scribble.
3. Press the blackened fingertip onto the sticky side of a piece of transparent tape.
4. Attach the tape to a piece of plain paper. You'll see a good clear print.

Tell the children that there are three basic types of fingerprints—whorls, arches, and loops. Let them examine the samples on Teaching Aid 6.3. Now let the children work to make all ten fingerprints and label them according to category type. Finally, make a class graph of right thumb prints on the graph grid from Teaching Aid 6.1. Interpret the graph with the class.

Evaluating the Activity: Note the children's cooperation, accuracy of classifying prints, and discussion of the graph results.

Extending the Activity: Encourage each child to fingerprint a family member and share the results with the class. Also let the children make toe prints, see what patterns they get, and compare toe prints with their fingerprints.

GRAB AND GRAPH

This activity has an element of suspense that makes children interested in the results. Children predict and then test predictions as they work with "grab and graph."

Objectives: Children will compare numbers of objects in "handfuls," graph results, and make predictions based on the data they gather. Children will work with the median of a set of data.

Materials: A large number of small objects (large dry lima beans, peanuts in the shell, small blocks or counters, or straws cut in thirds), a container with an opening large enough for children to reach in, paper to duplicate a graph grid from Teaching Aid 6.4.

Preparing for the Activity: Place the small objects in the container. Duplicate the graph form.

Approximate Time Frame: 20 to 30 minutes.

Conducting the Activity: Work in a small or large group. Show the children the object you have chosen to work with, and ask for an estimate of how many of the objects might be contained in a handful. Write several estimates on the chalkboard.

Have a child come up to the chalkboard and put the list of estimates in order from largest to smallest. Show the children how to choose the middle value—the median. If there is an odd number of estimates, the median may be found by alternately marking off numbers from each end of the list until only the middle value remains. If there is an even number of estimates, have the children simply state that the median is the number between the two middle values. For example, in the list made up of 8, 8, 9, 11, 12, and 14, the children should say: "The median is between 9 and 11."

Now let several children reach into the container and remove just one handful of the chosen object. Each child should count and report the number of objects in his or her handful. Have a student record the results on the chalkboard. Have another child put the results in order from largest to smallest and then determine the median.

If children grab handfuls of more than ten objects, have them record their numbers as tens and ones. If you are using straws as your chosen object, provide rubber bands for each child to bundle the straws in tens. Discuss the typical number of objects pulled from the container. If the children's initial predictions were very far from the actual results, encourage them to "re-predict" a more likely handful number.

Next, let the children help you in labeling the categories on the graph form. Now have each child pull out a handful of the small objects, count them, and make groups of ten wherever possible. Have the children take turns marking the number they grabbed from the container on the graph form. Discuss the results. If you are using peanuts as your chosen object, have the children predict the number of actual peanuts inside the shells—both the number in his or her own handful and the total number of all the peanuts. Then shell the peanuts and count them, grouping the total in hundreds, tens, and ones.

Evaluating the Activity: Observe the children as they count and group the small objects. See if they choose the correct graph categories. Note the children's ability to predict.

Extending the Activity: Let small groups of children work independently making graphs of handfuls of small objects, and then compare the results from group to group. Use different objects and repeat the experience.

MORE REUSABLE GRAPHS

These additional reusable graph formats will facilitate more valuable experiences in making and interpreting graphs.

Objectives: Children will make and interpret bar and picture graphs.

Materials: For the magnet graph: a small magnet (or piece of tape-on magnet strip) for each child, paper, steel cookie sheet, markers. For the posterboard graph: two pieces of posterboard, single-edged razor blade, paper clips. For the block graph: a classroom building block for each child, masking tape, markers, paper and markers for graph forms. For the bulletin board graph: bulletin board backing material (if desired), yarn or crepe paper to divide the bulletin board into sections, paper to make a graph title, category markers and graph markers, pins.

Preparing for the Activity: Gather and duplicate the materials for the kind of graph you wish to make. Teaching Aid 6.5 illustrates some samples.

Approximate Time Frame: 20 minutes per graph.

Conducting the Activity: Present the topic and categories for the graph you have selected. Invite the children to take turns placing their markers in the correct categories. Help the children interpret the graph by asking them to raise some questions about the graph and letting other students answer the questions.

Be sure the children compare the numbers of markers in the various categories and talk about the general impressions that the graph conveys. For instance, they may point out that all the categories are approximately equal or that one category was chosen much more often than any of the others. Let the children title the graph and attach their title to it.

Here are some reusable graph formats and topics:

Magnet Graph. Use a small magnet or piece of tape-on magnet strip for each child. Cut 5x5cm (2x2-inch) paper squares. Use a steel cookie sheet or stove pad for a graph board. Prepare category markers and blank markers for the graph's title. Let the children write their names on the squares and place them in the proper graph category, attaching them with the magnets.

Possible topics for the magnet graph include "Length of My Foot" (each child measures his or her right foot and then reports the length by entering it in the category of about 20cm, longer than 20cm, or shorter than 20cm) and "Number of Magnetic Objects in My Desk" (each child uses the magnet to see which objects attract, and then reports the number in categories of perhaps fewer than four, four, and more than four).

From *Exploring Mathematics: Activities for Concept and Skill Development*, Copyright © 1990 Scott, Foresman and Company.

Posterboard Graph. Use two sheets of posterboard to create a four-category graph form. Divide each category into 10x10cm (4x4-inch) squares. Leave room for category names and title. Slit the posterboard with a razor blade, and insert paper clips for the category names and title. Make category labels and a blank form for the topic you choose. Lay the graph on the floor, and let the children lay small objects on it.

Here are some topics you might try: "I Like to Write With . . ." (the children lay a pen, pencil, marker, or crayon in the correct category), and "I Found . . ." (hide small geometric shapes around the room, let each child collect one or two of them, and then have the children sort the objects on the graph form by shape).

Block Graph. Using classroom building blocks, let each child put a piece of masking tape on a block and write his or her name. Make the graph categories and leave a place for the title. Have the children pile their blocks in the appropriate category to make a vertical bar graph.

Try titles such as these: "A Good Snack" (offer choices of apples, cheese and crackers, and peanut butter sandwich), "Weather I Like" (categories might be hot, warm, cool, and cold), and "I'm Wearing . . ." (give the children choices such as jeans or other pants, belt or no belt, tennis shoes or other shoes).

Bulletin Board Graph. Divide a blank bulletin board into categories using crepe paper or thick yarn to make the divisions. Select graph categories and a topic. Prepare a blank paper for the title. Let the children make life-sized markers and take turns pinning them onto the bulletin board.

Some possible topics for the bulletin board graph include: "Around My Head" (let each child cut a paper strip to fit around his or her head and then pin the actual-sized strip onto the bulletin board), "Broad Jumps" (set up a place for the children to broad jump; then, as each one jumps, cut a strip of adding machine paper the length of the jump, and let the child label and pin the paper on the graph), and "Hand Graph" (have the children trace their hands on paper and then pin their tracings on the bulletin board in small, medium, and large categories).

Evaluating the Activities: Observe the children's abilities to make decisions and choose appropriate categories. Assess their discussion of the graph, noting who makes correct interpretations of the data shown. Also note who suggests appropriate titles for the completed graph.

Extending the Activities: Reuse the graph forms with topics suggested by the children. Where appropriate, ask the children to gather additional data at home and then add the data to the graphs begun at school.

$\div \times - + - \times \div$

CHAPTER

TEACHING

AIDS

Graph Title

Teaching Aid 6.1

Category Names

Reusable
Graphs

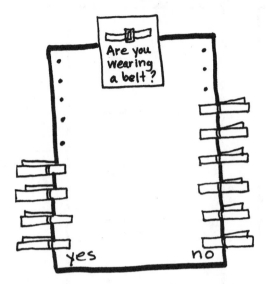

Are you wearing a belt?

yes   no

Clothespin Graph
Children mark their
choices with clothespins
in the proper category.
the dots guide them to
space the pins evenly.

Plain   Patterned   Our Tops

Stand-On Graph
Children sit or stand on
sections of paper or shelf
paper laid on the floor. Simply
change the title and captions
for reuse.

Teaching Aid 6.2a

DO YOU HAVE A PET?

yes   no

FELT FACE PATTERNS

MILK CARTON GRAPH MARKERS

Flatten the top of the carton. Tape it in place.

Cover the carton with two pieces of paper. Wrap the paper around. Tape it in place.

Tape on a photo or write your name on the carton.

Pile the milk carton markers up in categories or lay them flat on the floor.

Teaching Aid 6.2b

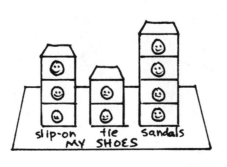

Steps for making fingerprints

1. Scribble with pencil onto paper.

2. Rub fingertip into scribble.

3. Press finger onto sticky side of tape.

4. Fasten tape onto white paper.

name _____

Fingerprint Names

arch

whorl

loop

Right Hand

Left Hand

Make a fingerprint on each finger. Compare your prints. Write the name of each print below it.

Teaching Aid 6.3

How Many are in a HANDFUL ?

Number of Objects in a Handful

Magnet Graph

Bits of magnet hold markers to a steel cookie sheet.

Block Graph

Children pile blocks on the form to show their choices.

Poster Board Graph

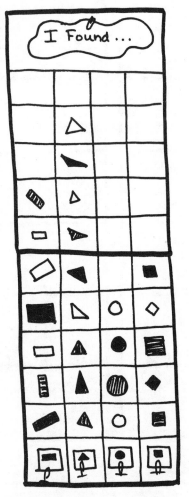

Children lay paper shapes in categories.

Bulletin Board Graph

Children pin actual-sized papers to the bulletin board.

Teaching Aid 6.5

From *Exploring Mathematics: Activities for Concept and Skill Development,* Copyright © 1990 Scott, Foresman and Company.

7

The Shape of Things: Geometry

Geometry is important in everyday life. People are surrounded by geometric shapes—some solid or three-dimensional, some flat or plane, and some points—that vary in size and proportions. In order to communicate effectively, people need to be able to describe, compare, and name the shapes in their environment. Early and effective teaching of the basic ideas of geometry also sets the stage for subsequent, more formal, work in the subject.

Building understanding requires that children have experiences with real materials and objects. In their study of geometry, young children should use real-world models, manipulatives, and pictures. They should compare geometric figures, discuss the figures' attributes, describe relationships among figures, and identify representations of a variety of figures. In addition, the children should constantly hear and use the vocabulary of geometry during these experiences.

The activities in this chapter provide a wide range of learning experiences in which children can handle materials and interact with what they are doing. Many of the activities are open-ended, encouraging experimentation, generation of many answers, and comparison of answers. Most of the activities feature a tactile aspect, thus making them especially appealing to young children.

3-D SHAPE SEARCH

This simple activity helps children become more aware of three-dimensional shapes in their environment.

Objectives: Children will examine, describe, and identify objects in their environment. They will work with regular prisms, cubes, cylinders, spheres, pyramids, and cones.

Materials: Classroom objects (you may wish to supplement with models of prisms, spheres, cubes, cylinders, pyramids, and cones), paper, pencils.

Preparing for the Activity: Look around your classroom and make sure that it contains at least an example or two of each geometric shape listed in the objectives.

Approximate Time Frame: 30 minutes.

Conducting the Activity: Let the children play "I Spy" as they find and discuss examples of each geometric solid. Have them take turns bringing smaller objects to show the group. List the objects the children find, along with some of each object's attributes, on the chalkboard or an experience chart. The children will probably find more examples of rectangular prisms than any other shape.

Count the faces (i.e., flat surfaces) and the angles or corners of several of the objects. Note that cylinders and spheres have no angles while pyramids have several angles and cones have just one point at the top. Let the children take turns tracing various object faces onto paper. Then they can cut out the resulting plane figures, hold them up, and compare their plane figures to the faces of the solid objects.

Evaluating the Activity: Observe which children are able to find examples of the figures and whether the children are able to discuss the properties of the objects they examined. Help those children who are less confident by working with them individually and by letting them hold and feel geometric solids as you talk about the shapes.

Extending the Activity: Ask each child to bring an example or two of geometric solids to class. Group and label the examples. Have the children cut apart empty containers, flatten their surfaces, and examine the various plane figures that make up the surface of a solid.

From *Exploring Mathematics: Activities for Concept and Skill Development,* Copyright © 1990 Scott, Foresman and Company.

YARN CLOSED CURVES

Children can easily arrange yarn to represent different geometric figures. Many children will "stay with" this activity because it has an appealing, sensory effect.

Objectives: Children will arrange yarn to represent various closed curves.

Materials: Flannel board, several pieces of heavy yarn, 15 to 20 push pins, paper to duplicate Teaching Aid 7.1a and b, scissors.

Preparing for the Activity: Gather supplies. Duplicate and cut apart the curve names.

Approximate Time Frame: 20 minutes.

Conducting the Activity: Show the children how to select a slip of paper that shows or names a closed curve; then arrange yarn on the flannel board for the shape. For polygons, instruct the children to select a push pin for each vertex, push the pins into the flannel board, and arrange the yarn around the pins to form the polygon. Let a small group of children work together; perhaps one child could make a figure and another child could "check" it.

Emphasize safety with the push pins, instructing the children that the pins should be used only in the flannel board and then returned to their container after use.

Evaluating the Activity: Spot-check the children's work. Ask them to name their figures and tell about pertinent characteristics of each curve. Observe which children handle the push pins responsibly.

Extending the Activity: Encourage the children to draw curves for their classmates to duplicate.

SHAPE WALKS

Using a variety of shape walks lets young children practice their skills in recognizing and naming geometric shapes. Shape walks are active and, therefore, appeal to young children.

Objectives: Children will recognize and name shapes in the environment.

Materials: For Shape Walk 1: paper and markers for signs, tape, scissors. For Shape Walk 2: colored construction paper, scissors. For Shape Walk 3: a long strip of paper (such as sentence strip paper or computer paper). For Shape Walk 4: masking tape, scissors, cloth for a blindfold.

Preparing for the Activities: Gather or duplicate materials as described for each shape walk.

Approximate Time Frame: 15 to 20 minutes per shape walk.

Conducting the Activities: Work on successive days with the different shape walks suggested below. When finished with all of them, let the children make a shape booklet. Each child can cut, label, and glue little shapes in a booklet.

Shape Walk 1: Shapes in the Environment. Encourage the children to identify geometric shapes in the classroom. They will probably find it easy to locate squares and rectangles, but they may have to look carefully for circles, triangles, ovals, and other geometric shapes.

Consider branching out from your classroom, taking your class on a walk around the school building or yard to locate more shapes. Instruct teams of children in advance to locate certain shapes you think they can find. For example, you might tell one team to look for glass squares, another to locate rectangles on the ground, and yet a third team to find circles above their heads. Make notes as you go along, and then summarize the results of your shape walk when you return to the classroom.

Shape Walk 2: Walk Across. Cut large paper shapes out of colored construction paper. Use different colors and sizes for different shapes. Lay the paper shapes in a pathway across the floor, and let the children take turns walking along the pathway as they follow your directions—e.g., "Walk along the pathway stepping only on rectangles," "Step on shapes with square corners," "Step only on the smaller shapes," "Walk along the pathway following this pattern: step on a shape with straight sides, one with a curvy shape, one with straight sides, curvy, and so on."

Once the children understand how to play the Walk Across game, let small groups play it independently.

Shape Walk 3: Walk 'n' Say. Using sentence strip paper, shelf paper, or computer paper, prepare a long strip of drawn geometric shapes. Hang the strip at the children's eye level. Show pairs of children how to

From *Exploring Mathematics: Activities for Concept and Skill Development,* Copyright © 1990 Scott, Foresman and Company.

walk along the strip, telling each other the names of the shapes and describing the shapes. Encourage the children to choose two or three shapes and discuss the similarities and differences among them.

If you post the shape walk strip near the place where the children line up, they will likely talk about it every time they get ready to leave the classroom.

Shape Walk 4: On the Floor. Use masking tape to outline large shapes on the floor. Encourage the children to walk around the shapes and discuss the various features of each one.

Later, divide the class into pairs. Blindfold one of the partners and let him or her be guided around a shape by the other. Then have each blindfolded child identify the shape he or she walked around and tell how he or she knew what shape it was.

Evaluating the Activities: Observe the children's participation, noting which children name shapes correctly and quickly and who follows directions well. Also note the children's cooperation and ability to help each other.

Extending the Activities: Ask the children to suggest other shape walk formats and, if possible, follow up on their suggestions. Use the *Walk 'n' Say* strip format to display numbers to read and basic facts problems to solve.

TEMPLATE FUN

This activity builds hand-eye coordination and reinforces the idea that polygons are the union of line segments.

Objectives: Children will use templates to draw polygons and circles. They will create pictures with polygons and circles, and they will make and extend patterns drawn with templates.

Materials: Plastic can lids, sharp-pointed scissors, fine-tip permanent marker or ballpoint pen, paper to duplicate task cards from Teaching Aid 7.2b, pencils or crayons.

Preparing for the Activities: Use plastic can lids to make templates. Trace the patterns for a circle and polygons from Teaching Aid 7.2a onto the lids with a permanent marker or ballpoint pen. Then use sharp-pointed scissors to puncture the lids and cut out the shapes. Label each shape as shown on Teaching Aid 7.2a, and duplicate the task cards from Teaching Aid 7.2b.

Approximate Time Frame: 30 minutes for each activity.

Conducting the Activities: Show the children how to hold the templates in place and outline the shapes with pencil or crayon. Use correct vocabulary as you work—e.g., a circle should be described as a set of points in the circle's outline, and each polygon is the set of points in the line segments that make up the polygon.

The children can trace the shapes with their crayons. Help the children identify the interiors and exteriors of the shapes. Use the word "region" to identify any shape and its interior. Have the children color some regions; for example, they could color a circle and its interior and call it a circular region. If they color a rectangle and its interior, they should call the result a rectangular region.

Have the children work with the following activities:

Exploration and Discussion. Have the children draw any shapes they like. Then divide the class into small groups, and have each group discuss, compare, and contrast their shapes. The children might even label some of their shapes.

Code Cards. Use the coded task cards from Teaching Aid 7.2b. Have the children choose cards and then use the cards to help draw what you tell them to draw.

Create a Picture. Invite the children to identify tasks and use templates to draw pictures. For example, a task might be to create a picture with five circles and then to add any details desired. Another task might be to draw several rectangles and then to turn each rectangle into a different design.

Extend the Pattern. Use the pattern task cards from Teaching Aid 7.2b. Let the children draw and continue the patterns suggested.

Evaluating the Activities: Check the children's abilities to use templates for drawing neat figures. From their discussion, assess their understanding of the names of shapes. Let students who need practice on names keep their shapes for future work.

Extending the Activities: Ask the children for ideas on how to use the templates for other math or art activities. Let the children make a shape book by drawing and labeling a different shape on each page. Invite the children to make and extend different patterns using the templates.

PUNCH-A-SHAPE

This activity strengthens hand-eye coordination. As children punch along the sides of geometric figures, they gain an understanding of the relationship between those sides and the final shape of the figure.

Objectives: Children will create geometric figures by punching along the sides of cardboard figures. They will display the "positives" and "negatives" of labeled geometric figures.

Materials: Posterboard, templates made from plastic lids, large nails (8-10cm, 3-4 inches, long), construction paper, scissors, glue.

Preparing for the Activity: Cut out several geometric shapes from posterboard or cardboard. Use these shapes to prepare templates by cutting the geometric shapes out of plastic lids (*see* "Template Fun" for details on this procedure).

Approximate Time Frame: 20 to 30 minutes.

Conducting the Activity: Show the children how to hold a shape firmly in place and use a nail to punch around its perimeter. Instruct the children to punch holes fairly close together—about .5cm (1/4 inch) apart. Encourage the children to notice how many sides they punch along and the kinds of angles each figure has.

  After they punch around a figure, the children should gently punch it out. They can glue the punched shape—the "positive"—on a sheet of contrasting color and then place it next to the hole (the "negative") left in the paper. Instruct the children to label each shape.

" Positive"

"Negative"

  The punch-a-shapes make an interesting and attractive bulletin board display.

Evaluating the Activity: Note each child's ability to hold the figures in place while punching along the sides. Check to be sure each child's shapes are correctly labeled.

Extending the Activity: Let the children punch along large numeral cutouts and then punch the correct number of holes for each numeral. For a project, have the children punch around seasonal shapes—leaves, pumpkins, hearts, etc.

÷ × − + − × ÷

CHAPTER

7

TEACHING

AIDS

÷ × − + − × ÷

From *Exploring Mathematics: Activities for Concept and Skill Development*, Copyright © 1990 Scott, Foresman and Company.

triangle	circle	diamond (rhombus)
square	triangle with 1 right angle	oval
rectangle	shape with 4 sides (quadrilateral)	triangle with 2 equal sides

Teaching Aid 7.1a

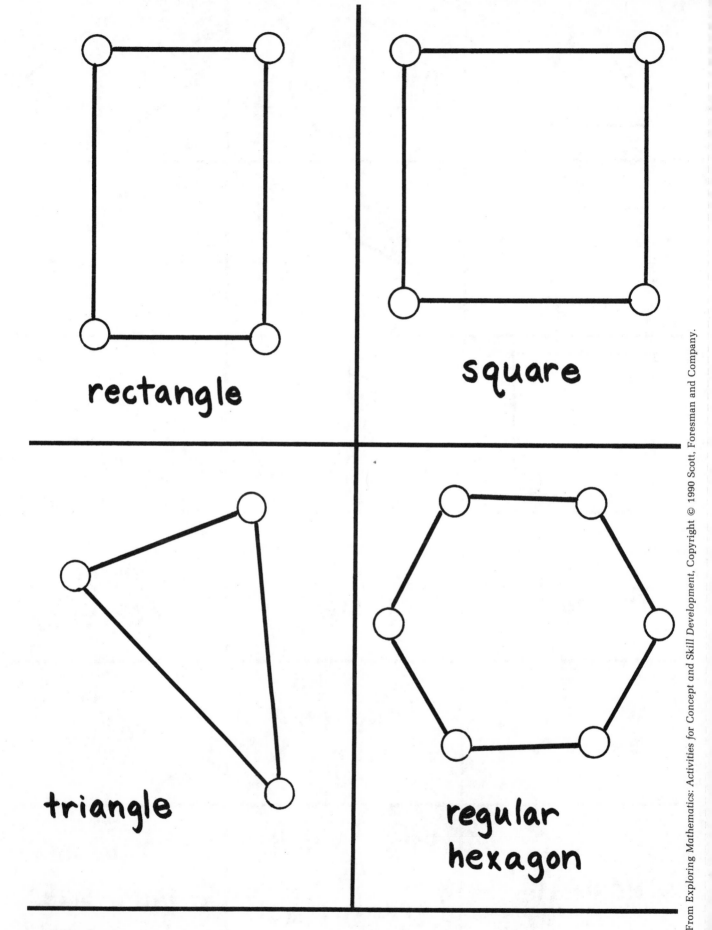

rectangle

square

triangle

regular
hexagon

From *Exploring Mathematics: Activities for Concept and Skill Development*, Copyright © 1990 Scott, Foresman and Company.

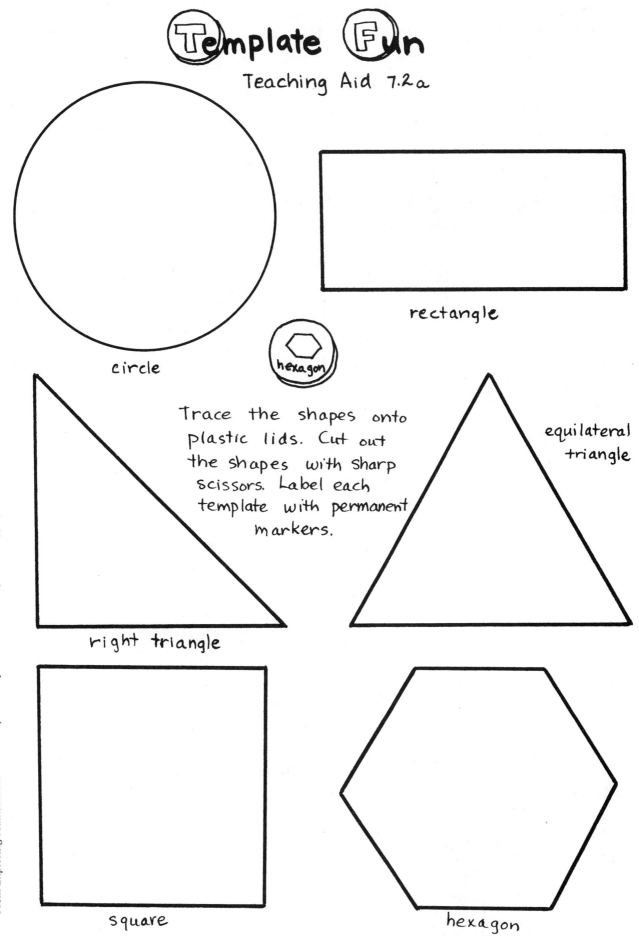

Template Fun

Teaching Aid 7.2a

circle

rectangle

hexagon

Trace the shapes onto plastic lids. Cut out the shapes with sharp scissors. Label each template with permanent markers.

equilateral triangle

right triangle

square

hexagon

Template Fun
Teaching Aid 7.2 b

For the first 5 cards, children choose a card, then draw what the "instructions" say.

For the pattern cards, the children draw and continue the patterns.

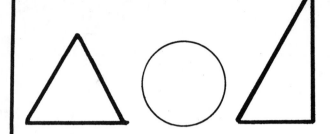

2
1

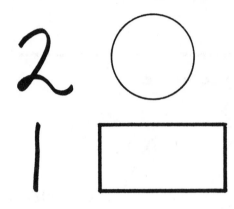

4
3

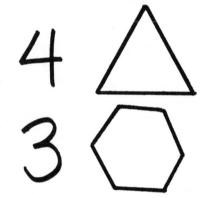

2 squares
5 circles

3 hexagons
4 rectangles

Draw and continue the patterns.

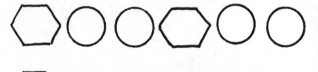

Draw and continue the patterns.

From *Exploring Mathematics: Activities for Concept and Skill Development,* Copyright © 1990 Scott, Foresman and Company.

8
How Big? How Heavy?: Measurement for Young Children

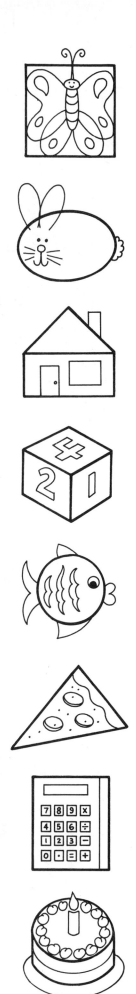

Through concrete experiences, children build their ideas of the processes of measurement and their appreciation of people's need to measure. For measurement to be meaningful to young children, they must make comparisons of lengths, volumes, and masses (weights). Children must build mental images of standard units of measurement and then use these images to compare and estimate physical objects.

Length is the easiest measurement for young children; by the second or third grade, they can master the use of a simple ruler. Although they find measurements of volume and mass more difficult, children can deal with these too if the concepts are presented in natural and meaningful ways. Moreover, early experiences with volume and mass provide a strong foundation for mastery of these topics in the middle grades.

The activities in this chapter utilize metric measurements. Why metrics? In addition to their worldwide acceptance, metric measurements play a major role in the science and mathematics curricula of the upper grades as well as in the scientific and medical professions. The metric system is more logically sound than the customary "inch-pound" measurement system; and since metric units are based on tens, hundreds, and thousands, learning the metric system complements the study of place value.

Teachers who prefer to use customary measurements—or want to present both systems of measurement to their students—will find that they must make only minor adjustments to the following activities.

METRIC ME

Completing the "Metric Me" booklet offers children several experiences with measuring length and an opportunity to measure mass too. The results are especially meaningful because the booklet is personalized.

Objectives: Children will estimate and measure length and mass; they will record results in a personalized booklet.

Materials: Paper to duplicate booklets from Teaching Aid 8.1a and b, four tape measures, masking tape, several 20-30cm rulers, one or two tape measures for measuring heads, step-on scale.

Preparing for the Activity: Duplicate a "Metric Me" booklet for each child, with the pages running back-to-back. Set up the tape measures as shown so that the children can measure their height and arm span. Set out the rulers, tapes for measuring heads, and step-on scale for the children to use.

Approximate Time Frame: 15 minutes for each page of the booklet.

Conducting the Activity: Pass out the "Metric Me" booklets. Have the children fold them to make four little pages. Instruct the children to write their names on the front (one letter per space), and then determine how many centimeters long their names are.

   Show the children how to help each other measure height and arm span. For height, show them where the 100cm mark is on the tape measure. Ask them to compare several classmates' heights (before measuring), compare the heights to the 100cm distance, and then estimate the heights. Emphasize that while an estimate is a guess rather than a measurement, it can be a good guess if compared accurately to a known distance. Show the children how to stand in order to measure arm span and how to help each other read the distance of each arm span.

From *Exploring Mathematics: Activities for Concept and Skill Development,* Copyright © 1990 Scott, Foresman and Company.

Outline the other tasks on the first three pages of the booklet. Let the children proceed, working in twos and threes to complete the pages. You will probably need to instruct each group separately in how to read their masses (or weights) from the step-on scale.

After they finish their measurements, have the children compare data. You will probably not be able to check the accuracy of each child's measurements, but be sure to spot-check answers for reasonableness and completeness.

Finally, take the children to an area where they can perform the physical tasks called for on the fourth page of the booklet. Let the children work in groups of two or three to finish this page, but make sure that each child records his or her measurements.

After they finish recording all their data, the students may complete the face on the cover of their booklets. They should then take their "Metric Me" booklets home to share with their parents. Children in kindergarten and first grade will probably need a good deal of help to complete the booklet, and you should plan to proceed one page at a time with these younger students.

Evaluating the Activity: Did each child complete the booklet? Were their estimates and answers reasonable? Did the children help each other make and check measurements?

Extending the Activity: Let the children make similar measurements of at least one family member and share their results with the class. Ask the children to suggest other kinds of measurements they might include in their "Metric Me" booklets. Use some of the children's suggestions to add two to four pages to the booklet. Then choose one or more of these supplemental measurements and analyze and graph the results for the class. For instance, you might ask the children to record the widths of their handprints on the chalkboard. Put the widths in order from largest to smallest, look at the range of measurements, and pick a typical value—the median or middle value. Choose some intervals for a bar graph, and then let each child fill in a block on the graph.

SHOW ME A LENGTH

This quick and easy game will build children's mental images of length measurements.

Objectives: Children will use their hands to show length measurements.

Materials: A ruler for each child or pair of children.

Approximate Time Frame: 5 to 10 minutes.

Conducting the Activity: Play "Show Me" for just five to ten minutes. Start by having each child lay a ruler on the desk or table but look at you. Demonstrate how to show lengths—such as 2cm or 8cm—as a distance between thumb and index finger. Demonstrate how to show longer distances—20cm or 45cm—between the fingertips of both hands.

Then have the children look around and compare the lengths they are showing with other lengths. They should look at their rulers only *after* their hands are "set." Now call out various distances—7cm, 2cm, 20cm, 10cm, etc.—and have the children use their hands to show the distances based on their mental images of certain distances before moving their hands near their rulers to check themselves.

Evaluating the Activity: Note the speed with which the children can show the measurements. Make mental notes about whose measurements seem reasonable and who needs more practice and help. Let the children who need more practice work with their classmates.

Extending the Activity: Play the "Show Me" game with inches. Show the children a length and have them write down an estimate. Check estimates after each four or five problems and accept the reasonable answers.

MEASURE AND EAT

Children usually find that measuring becomes a very practical matter when there are recipes to be made and enjoyed.

Objectives: Groups of children will work together and measure as they prepare a recipe.

Materials: For the Butterfly Nectar: milk, banana, cinnamon, ice cubes, blender. For the Trail Mix: coconut, chocolate chips, raisins, peanuts, small plastic bags. For each recipe: measuring cups and spoons, paper to duplicate recipes, crayons or markers, laminating material (optional).

Preparing for the Activities: Choose a recipe and secure the ingredients (parents might be willing to contribute recipe ingredients) and the necessary equipment. Duplicate a recipe from Teaching Aid 8.2a or b. Color and (if desired) laminate the recipe.

Approximate Time Frame: 10 to 20 minutes per recipe.

Conducting the Activities: Work with a small group of children, letting them take turns measuring ingredients and completing the steps in the recipe. Share the food with the entire class. In addition, you should discuss the nutritional value of each recipe's ingredients, and you might let the children mark down their feelings about the recipe on a graph form.

Here some special features worth noting about each recipe:

Butterfly Nectar. As you study insects, you might want to spend some time examining the beautiful, intriguing butterfly. This easy recipe becomes even more interesting when children learn that butterflies sip nectar from flowers with a long trunk-like organ called a proboscis. Plan to make this recipe in spring or fall when real butterflies are available for observation. Let the children sip the nectar through straws.

Trail Mix. Plan a walking field trip or nature hike. Then let a small group of students make a bag of trail mix for each class member. Pack up the individual bags and then distribute them at an appropriate resting spot in your walk.

Evaluating the Activities: Observe the children and see if they use the measuring tools skillfully, read the recipe accurately, and work cooperatively.

Extending the Activities: Make other recipes. Talk about doubling or halving recipes to make larger or smaller amounts. Help the children learn how each recipe's ingredients are grown or produced. Help the children read the nutrition information on the ingredient packages.

MAKE ME BALANCE

Before they are ready to use a balance scale to determine the masses of objects, children must have experience in manipulating the scale to see how it works.

Objectives: Children will place objects on both sides of a balance scale in order to make the scale balance. They will try a number of different combinations of materials, verifying and recording the results of each combination.

Materials: Balance scale, paper to duplicate charts from Teaching Aid 8.3, small objects (e.g., crayons, Styrofoam bits, paper clips, pennies or nickels, plastic counters, beans, small rocks).

Preparing for the Activity: Duplicate copies of Teaching Aid 8.3. Each group will need at least one form.

Approximate Time Frame: 20 minutes.

Conducting the Activity: Show a group of children how the balance scale works. Place an object on one side of the scale, and point out how that side goes lower. Now show the children another object and ask them to predict what will happen when you place that object on the other side of the scale. Then place the object on the other side and let the children see what happens: A heavier object on the second side makes that side go down while a lighter object allows the first side to stay down. If the object on the second side has approximately the same mass as the first object, the sides of the scale will balance.

Let the children try placing different objects on the balance scale, predict what will happen, and then make statements about the relationships of the objects' masses. Show the group how to record the data for their objects, and then let them proceed to manipulate the scale and record their results.

Rotate the groups so that all the students have an opportunity to use the balance scale. Then gather the class in one large group to review everyone's results.

Evaluating the Activity: Observe the children's ability to predict what will happen when various objects are placed on the balance scale. Spot-check the children's forms for accurate recording of data. See who works cooperatively.

Extending the Activity: Invite the children to bring small objects to place on the balance scale. Introduce the idea of standard weights used on one side of the scale to determine the weight of objects placed on the other side. Guide children to determine the masses of small classroom objects: crayons, pencils, rulers, etc.

From *Exploring Mathematics: Activities for Concept and Skill Development*, Copyright © 1990 Scott, Foresman and Company.

FISHING FUN

Children love to catch paper fish, using a magnet for bait! This is a versatile and attractive learning activity because once the fish are caught, they can be used for many purposes.

Objectives: Children will catch paper fish, compare their sizes, and put them in order by length. Children will estimate and measure fish lengths.

Materials: Paper to duplicate fish patterns from Teaching Aid 8.4a and b, laminating material, paper clips, string, magnet, blue construction paper (optional), rulers and meter sticks.

Preparing for the Activities: Duplicate the fish patterns. You will want at least two pages of each pattern for a small group of children. Laminate the fish patterns, cut them out, and fasten a paper clip to the mouth of each fish. Tie a magnet on the end of the string. If you wish, you can create a "pond" for the fish out of a large sheet of blue construction paper.

Approximate Time Frame: 15 to 20 minutes per activity.

Conducting the Activities: Have a group of children lay the fish on the "pond" or on the floor or a table top. Instruct them to take turns catching the fish and doing one of more of the following activities:

Ordering. Each child puts his or her caught fish in order from longest to shortest. Then two children "merge" their fish and work cooperatively to put them in order by size. When more than one fish of a given size is caught, tell the children to lay one fish atop the other.

Estimating and Measuring. Each child estimates the lengths of his or her caught fish, records the estimate, and then measures the fish and records the measurements on the form (Teaching Aid 8.4a). In the third column of the form, the children analyze their estimates.

Making a Meter of Fish. Have the children work in two teams. One team catches fish and lays them above the meter stick. The other team catches fish and lays them below the meter stick. The two teams take turns catching fish until both complete a meter's length of fish.

You might have the children record a number sentence to show (and check) how they made a meter's length. For example, if a team caught three 10cm fish, four 8cm fish, two 3cm fish, and one each of 9cm, 6cm, 5cm, and 12cm fish, the children could record the following sentence:

$$10 + 10 + 10 + 8 + 8 + 8 + 8 + 3 + 3 + 9 + 6 + 5 + 12 = 100.$$

Evaluating the Activities: Observe the children to see that they work cooperatively and order their fish correctly. Spot-check their estimates and measurements to make sure that their answers are reasonable.

Extending the Activities: Write numbers on the fish with crayon or water-based marker. Let the children take turns catching fish and reading their numbers. Then write problems on the fish and repeat the procedure. If the children can answer their problems correctly, let them keep the fish. If they answer incorrectly, they must put their fish back in the pond and try again. Wipe off the numbers/problems when you are finished.

From *Exploring Mathematics: Activities for Concept and Skill Development*, Copyright © 1990 Scott, Foresman and Company.

÷ ✕ − ✛ − ✕ ÷

CHAPTER

8

TEACHING

AIDS

÷ ✕ − ✛ − ✕ ÷

• METRIC ME BOOKLET •

Your Name -- Fill in one square per letter.

How many cm long is your name?

my age _____

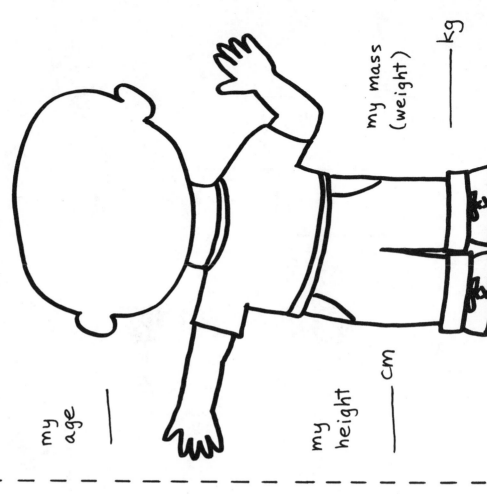

my height _____ cm

my mass (weight) _____ kg

Outdoor Measures

my broadjump _____ cm

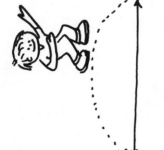

my giant step _____ cm

the time it took me to run the 30 meter dash _____ seconds

- 4 -   Teaching Aid 8.1 a

My Handprint

Trace your hand here. Measure its length and width.

- 3 -

Some Special Measures

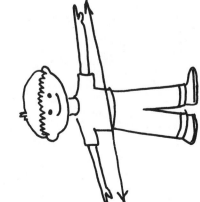

my armspan
_____ cm

length of my shoe _____ cm

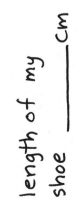

my mouth when I'm serious
_____ cm

my mouth in a big grin
_____ cm

- 2 -

BUTTERFLY NECTAR

Measure into blender:

375 mℓ milk

1 small banana

1.25 mℓ cinnamon

4 ice cubes

Whirl mixture until smooth.
Pour into 4 small cups.
Sip "butterfly style" from
a straw "proboscis."

Teaching Aid 8.2a

TRAIL MIX

Spoon into a baggie:

10 ml coconut

10 ml chocolate chips

15 ml raisins

15 ml peanuts

Shake the baggie.

Munch as you walk.

MAKE ME BALANCE

" 3 crayons balance 12 styrofoam bits."

_____ balances _____

_____ balances _____

_____ balances _____

_____ balances _____

_____ balances _____

_____ has a greater mass than _____

_____ has a smaller mass than _____

_____

Fill in your own statement here.

Teaching Aid 8.3

FISHING FUN Fish Patterns

Recording Form
Fill in the chart as you catch fish.

Estimated Length	Actual Length	How Close Was Your Estimate?		
		Larger than Actual	Smaller than Actual	About the Same

Teaching Aid 8.4a

☆FISHING☆ ☆FUN☆ More Patterns

Teaching Aid 8.4b

From Exploring Mathematics: Activities for Concept and Skill Development, Copyright © 1990 Scott, Foresman and Company.